Learn Perl 1 – Course Book

Learn Perl 1

By Greg Boug

International Standard Book Number: 978-1-84799-260-4

First Edition, November 2007

Trademarks

All terms mentioned in this book that are known to be trademarks have been appropriately capitalized. The publisher and the author cannot attest to the accuracy of this information. Use of a term in this book should not be regarded as affecting the validity of any trademark or service mark.

Table of Contents

Introduction

Course Objectives

This course is designed to provide a basic introduction to programming using Perl 5. It does not assume any prior knowledge of programming; however knowledge of languages such as C will help.

This course is designed to run in either of two ways. If you are a novice programmer with no experience, you should start at topic 1 and work through from there. If you have programmed in other languages before, you can optionally start working from chapter 5. You should still read through the first 4 chapters, as any new language can introduce new ideas that you had not thought of before. Perl is certainly no exception to this.

This course will teach responsible Perl programming. As Perl is often criticized for producing "unreadable code", care must be taken by the programmer to ensure that the code is cleanly written, so that it can be extended at a later date as required. Some of the exercises are designed to emphasize this point. The exercises are designed to be run sequentially, and you will often revisit exercises and expand upon them.

Assumed Knowledge

This course assumes that you have at least some basic programming knowledge. I.e. you understand what a variable is, what a loop is and other basic concepts such as these. If you do not have this knowledge, it is advised that you research basic programming concepts prior to attempting this course. Knowledge of another programming language such as C, Java or another scripting language will be of benefit.

Course Requirements

This course does not make any assumptions about what platform you are using to learn Perl on. This course can be run on either a Windows™ or Unix™ based environment.

In either case, you will need access to the following:

- A copy of Perl – version 5.8 or later (version 5.10 is preferred for some new features)
- Either of:
    - an *Integrated Development Environment* (IDE) or
    - a text editor
- Access to a database (e.g. MySQL) as well as the installation of the Perl DBI and DBD::mysql modules.

Examples of IDE's could include commercial applications such as ActiveState's Komodo IDE (available from http://www.activestate.com/),

Whilst larger Perl projects may benefit from the use of an IDE, it is not essential. A simple text editor is all that is required to produce small scripts. Text editors as Vi (or Vim), Emacs offer features such as syntax highlighting and other features that are beneficial to programming in general. Editors such as notepad can still be used, but lack the functionality required for more complex programming. Notepad should serve as a bare minimum for editing code for this course.

For later topics, access to a small database is required. One suggestion is the freely available MySQL. This is available from http://www.mysql.com/. This is the suggested database for this course, as it provides a simple setup and configuration, as well as a connection interface that is simple to connect to with both the Windows™ and UNIX ™ operating systems. Of course, other databases can be used in place; however the database connections (as well as the sample data) are left as an exercise to the reader in these cases. Sample data for exercises can be obtained from the website for this course, or from your instructor.

Obtaining Perl

Depending on the platform being used, Perl can be obtained from a number of sources. In Unix™ and Linux operating systems, it can be downloaded from http://www.perl.com/, and is available in both source code and binary formats. For Windows™ users, there are a couple of options. Firstly, there is the option to compile the source code (the download page has links to support information about how to compile under Windows™. Another option is to use the Cygwin environment available from http://www.cygwin.com/.

The other (possibly better) option for Windows™ is to use ActivePerl™. This can be downloaded from http://www.activestate.com/. This method provides an installation utility as well as a graphical package manager for installing additional Perl modules.

Course Website

Copies of materials used in this book are available from http://www.gbunixtraining.com/. This material includes any data files required to work with the exercises. Also, sample solutions are available from the website.

Topic 1 – Introduction to Perl

Overview

This topic will give an introduction to the Perl scripting language, including history and background. You will also be introduced to some basic scripts, as well as how to run them in both a Windows and UNIX environment.

Topic Objectives

This first topic is meant to give you an introductory view into what Perl is, what it does, as well as give you an overview of how to create your own scripts.

By the end of this topic, you will be able to:

- Understand Perl's history, including an appreciation of its background

- Create a trivial script and run it

- Understand the basic methods of executing Perl scripts in both a Unix and Windows™ environment

Brief history of Perl

Perl was originally designed by Larry Wall in 1987. The initial revision released in December 1987 was intended as a text processing language – largely a merging of C, Awk, Sed and some other shell concepts. Originally titled Pearl, until it was found that there was already another language with the same name; it was renamed to Perl prior to its initial release.

Perl often stands for *"Practical Extraction and Report Language"*, which is a fancy way of saying that the language was originally oriented towards parsing information in a text form, and either making modifications to it or building reports based on it.

Larry Wall once suggested that Perl really stood for *"Pathologically Eclectic Rubbish Lister"*; however the name was not intended to have any expansions.

One of the underlying philosophies of Perl is that there must be "more than one way to do it". You will note throughout this book that whilst certain methods of writing Perl code may exist – and that there are multiple ways to tackle any issue. The reasoning behind this is that programmers think in different ways, so for the language to be useful, it must be able to cater to those different schools of thought. As a result, you will find structured programming ideas, Object-oriented concepts, as well as other aspects that arose from its shell scripting history.

Perl has since gone through a number of revisions. The current at time of writing is version 5.10. Versions 1-3 were not particularly widespread, in fact it wasn't until version 4 that some operating systems included it in their core distribution. Version 5 of Perl introduced a more modular means of programming in Perl, which meant that Object-oriented programming techniques could now be used. This process has been refined somewhat since it was introduced

Ultimately, Perl is a scripting language, which means that the code is not put into any compiled format. There are tools in existence to do this, however they are largely commercial products. There is a Perl compiler in the core distribution, `perlcc`, however this does not provide any form of optimization – it merely pushes everything required into a copy of the Perl interpreter.

Running Perl Scripts

Under Windows, running Perl scripts can be achieved by either double clicking on the script (when the file association under windows for .pl files is set to run Perl, as it is when ActivePerl™ is installed), or you can run the script by running the interpreter as follows:

```
C:\perl\scripts>perl -w script.pl
```

Note that in this case, you have to specify all the Perl command line switches you need to use, which can make running some scripts more difficult.

Under Linux and Unix™ there are also two means of running Perl scripts provided by the operating system. The first is the same as the second method for Windows (running it as 'perl script.pl'). The other is to make the script executable using this command:

```
$ chmod 755 script.pl
```

Then use the UNIX #! line to specify Perl as the interpreter.

The UNIX ™ #! Line

Under UNIX™, there is a facility for executing text files using an interpreter. When a program is executed within UNIX, the first few characters are checked to determine what type of executable it is. For text scripts such as Perl (or Bourne Shell, Python, etc.) the operating system will check the first two characters in the file to be #!. If they are, then the rest of the first line explains what interpreter to use. In our case, we want it to be Perl. So to run Perl, place the following *at the very start of the file*:

```
#!/usr/bin/perl -w
```

Now, this assumes that Perl is located in /usr/bin. If this is not the case, you will need to adjust this line to contain the full path to where Perl is installed.

It is important to ensure that this line is the very first line of the script, as UNIX will only look at the first few characters of the file to determine what type of executable it is.

Note also the use of -w. The interpreter line here allows for the ability to command line switches to the script execution. In this case, -w enables warnings, which will cause the interpreter to print out warning messages when things are not working as planned. We will cover this in more detail in topic 11.

If you do not know the location of Perl, or it is going to vary on systems you intend to run this script on, there is another option. You can make use of the env command, which will source a standard environment to run a command – in this case, we want it to run Perl. Take a look at this example:

```
#!/usr/bin/env perl -w
```

This will result in a small overhead of running the env utility as well, but this will source the users' environment (including their PATH environment) and attempt to use this to run Perl. The downside of this is that it will use whichever installation of Perl occurs first in the users' path – so take care when using it. This is especially true if you have Perl modules installed from CPAN that are installed for use with a specific installation of Perl.

Some sample scripts

The simplest script is the hello world script. This is a script that is done in every language as a first step so that you gain an understanding of how the process works of writing a script. The text for the script is as follows:

```
#!/usr/bin/perl -w
print "Hello world\n";
```

When you attempt to run a Perl command, the first thing the interpreter will do is check the script to ensure that it is valid Perl code. If it isn't, you will see something like this printed:

```
syntax error at script.pl line 3, near "print"
err.pl had compilation errors.
```

This is essentially the same as with any other programming language. You will need to go through your code (in this case, to line 3) and fix the syntax error.

Here is a more complex example of Perl code. Don't worry if you can't understand it yet. This script introduces a few concepts that not yet been discussed. It is intended that this script give you an idea of how Perl scripts can be set out. As there is more than one way to do it, this is only one way of writing Perl code to perform this task.

```
#!/usr/bin/perl -w
# Additional Perl module to enforce some stricter variable checking
use strict;

# Open the file sales.csv and handle what happens if the file can't
# be opened correctly.
open FH, "sales.csv" or die "Unable to read sales.csv: $!\n";
my $total = 0;

# We will read through the entire file here and sum up the total sales.
# Assuming here that the sale price is the second field in the CSV file.
while (my $line = <FH>) {
      chomp $line;
      my @data = split(",", $line);
      $total += $data[1];
}
# Close the file, since we no longer need it.
close FH;
print "Sales total: \$" . sprintf("%.02f", $total) . "\n";
exit;
```

This script introduces you to a basic loop structure (we will cover in more detail in topic 4), arrays (covered in topic 5), and some file handling (covered in topic 3)

Commenting Perl Code

All programming languages require the ability to comment code. Perl provides two mechanisms, comments and "perldoc", which is a format for embedding documentation into your Perl code. We will cover perldoc at a later stage, but for now, here is how commenting works within Perl.

```
# Display the words "Hello world"
print "Hello world\n";
```

Essentially, commenting in Perl is done on a single line, beginning with '#'. Anywhere from the '#' to the end of the line will be considered as a comment. It does not have to be at the start of the line; however it should generally not be done mid-statement. The following examples are also ways of commenting in Perl:

```
print "Hello World\n"; # display "Hello World"
```

As with all commenting, it should be done in terms of explaining what the code is meant to be doing. So therefore, doing something like this isn't very useful:

```
$i++; # increment i
```

Any programmer can pick up the fact that the variable $i is being incremented here. Something more useful would be something like:

```
# Run through for each of the 10 fields in the array
while ($i < 10) {
        $i++;
        print $array[$i];
}
```

In this example, we provide more useful information to someone who comes along later to read the code already written. Comments should always be written with the idea of using them to explain to another programmer (or yourself!) what you were trying to achieve when you wrote this piece of code.

Exercise 1.2 – Commenting Code

1. Copy the script ex-1.1.pl into ex-1.2.pl

2. In ex-1.2.pl, place some comments into the code above the existing code, for example:

   ```
   #!/usr/bin/perl -w
   # This is the hello world program.
   print "Hello World\n";
   ```

3. Now run ex-1.2.pl and notice that the comments are ignored when running the script.

Available Documentation Resources

Perl provides a substantial amount of documentation in the form of "man" pages. Under UNIX, type 'man perl' to get the index page. This will give a list of other documentation man pages that are available.

Under the ActiveState™ Perl installation, there is a HTML version of this documentation. Once ActivePerl™ is installed; simply go to the Documentation link inside the start menu. On the left pane, scroll down to the section "Perl Core Documentation" and start with the link named 'Perl', this provides an index page to the rest of the core documentation.

This documentation is also available online at http://perldoc.perl.org/.

Summary

We have seen the origins of Perl, which gives an idea of what the language was originally designed to do. In addition, you have now seen some basic Perl scripts, and while you may not yet fully understand them yet, you may see some similarities with other programming languages you have come across.

Perl can be a complex language, allowing you to perform complex tasks with a smaller amount of coding effort compared to a lot of traditional styled languages such as C or Java.

Review Questions

1. What was Perl originally designed to do?

   _____

   _____

   _____

   _____

   _____

2. How do you run a script under UNIX?

   _____

   _____

   _____

   _____

   _____

3. When commenting code under any language, what sort of things should you put in comments for?

   _____

   _____

   _____

   _____

   _____

Topic 2 – Perl Variables

Overview

Scalar values form the basis of data within Perl. Scalars in Perl have no type, so they can hold any single piece of data. This topic shows how single values of data are handled within Perl and starts to introduce you to the structure of Perl variables.

Topic Objectives

By the end of this topic, you will be able to:

- Understand how Perl treats individual pieces of data using a scalar value

- Define, manipulate and report scalar values

- Gain an appreciation for some of the internal functions that work with scalars

- Gain an appreciation of some of the internal scalar values that are available for use within Perl

Scalar Variables

In Perl, the common unit of data is called a scalar value. Scalar values hold essentially a single value of data. It can be a number (integer or float), a character, a string, a reference.

Perl is a type-less language, so a single value has no concept of being an integer, floating point number or other similar construct like you will find in languages such as C.

In Perl, for any single value the variable is denoted by a $ followed by the variable name, for example $foo. Here are some example definitions:

```
$a = 1; # Defining an integer
$b = "hello"; # Defining a string
$b = 5.3; # A floating point number
$c = 'another string'; # Defining another string
```

At this point, you may think "but I just assigned a string to $b. Isn't that bad?" The answer to that question is "*maybe*". As far as strict Perl code is concerned – it doesn't matter. You can change between strings, numbers or any other type of data that can be stored in a scalar value. Perl takes care of this for you.

However there is the issue of reading your code later to consider. In some cases, it is perfectly OK to overwrite variables with different type information. One such example would be when using variables as temporary storage, such as an iterator.

One of the key things to remember with Perl is that it will always try to make the best of what you tell it to do. It will attempt to make sense of what you say, which in some cases isn't what you intended.

Strings in Perl

Perl has a number of different ways to define a string within a scalar. You define these methods using different types of quotes. A simple string which contains no extra processing is done via single quotes. For example:

```
$simple = 'the quick brown fox';
```

This will take the literal string and store it into the scalar. It will do no processing whatsoever.

The next type is the more common; it allows an amount of processing to be done on the string prior to storing it in the scalar. It will substitute variables, special escaped characters and so on. An example would be:

```
$complex = "$simple jumped over the lazy dog\n";
```

Note two things about the line of code you just saw. The first one is that we were able to do a string substitution into the new string, so the contents of $simple will be put in at the start of the string.

The second thing to note is the \n at the end. This is a special character that Perl will interpret as a newline character. There are a number of other characters you can us in this fashion. Here is a table with some of the more commonly used ones:

Special Character	Effect
\n	New line
\r	Carriage return (required for Windows systems with a new line)
\t	Tab character

Table 1 - Special characters

The third method you can use is a more complex one. It allows you to run an external command and store the contents of STDOUT into a string. To do this, we use 'back ticks'. An example would be:

```
$run = `/usr/bin/env`;
```

This will run the /usr/bin/env command and store the output into $run. Note that this can also be done with arrays. We will cover the effects of assigning this to an array in a later chapter.

Manipulating Scalar Values

Once stored, there are a number of ways to manipulate scalar values. Looking first at numerical values, it is possible to do simple mathematical calculations using a notation similar to many languages you may have come across. Here are some examples:

```
$a = 4 + 3;
$b = 48 / 12;
$c = $a * $b;
$d = 5 * ($c - 5);
```

As you can see from these examples, Perl follows a fairly standard means of assigning new values to scalars. Remember each time you refer to a scalar value in Perl, you must put a $ sign on the front. It has special meaning to tell the Perl interpreter that the variable you wish to deal with is in fact a scalar value. There are other symbols for arrays, hashes, etc. that we will cover later.

Special Operators

Now that you have seen some of the basics of assigning and manipulating scalars, let's have a look at some of the other special operators you can do when manipulating strings and numbers in Perl. Take a look at the following examples:

```
$a = $a + 1;
$b = $b + 3;
$c = $c * 5;
$d = "Hello";
$d = "$d world";
```

These are fairly straightforward mathematical and string manipulations. However, Perl permits the use of a few shorthand techniques. The first is the same as you may have seen in languages such as C. It is possible to use of the ++ operator to increment a scalar value. It works in the same was as in C. Take a look at these examples:

```
$a = 0;
$a++;
print "$a\n";
$a--;
print "$a\n";
```

Note that there is also a decrement operator, which works to subtract one from the value of the variable being used.

The next shorthand operator you can use is essentially an extension on the idea of the increment operator. It serves to work when you want to add more than one to an existing variable. For example, this may be useful when calculating a total. Here is an example of how it may be used:

```
$total += $a;
```

In this example, we are adding the value of $a to $total, and would be the same as writing $total = $total + $a. Note that you can do any operator here, such as:

```
$a /= 5; # $a = $a / 5
$b *= 2; # $b = $b * 2
```

Note that is works for any operator within Perl, not just numeric operators. It also works for operators such as the string concatenate operator. Take a look at this example:

```
$simple = $simple . " jumped over the lazy dog\n";
```

This is a simple way of joining two strings together. Another way to write this code would be:

```
$simple .= " jumped over the lazy dog\n";
```

Basically, this tells the reader to add this new string onto the end of the original string, in this case, $simple.

Exercise 2.2 – More advanced string and numeric manipulation

1. Write a Perl script, call it ex-2.2.pl. Put the following code in:

   ```
   #!/usr/bin/perl
   $string = "This is a test";
   print $string * 5;
   ```

2. Run this script. Have a look at the output. Was it what you expected? Run the script again but this time through add in the –w flag to the #! line.

3. Write another Perl script, ex-2.3.pl that calculates the cost of buying 3 items entered in from the keyboard. It will get input from a prompt like this (replace the XXX.XX with the actual total from the three items):

   ```
   Enter price of item 1:
   Enter price of item 2:
   Enter price of item 3:
   The total cost is $XXX.XX
   ```

Functions working with scalars

In addition to working with operators, Perl has some internally defined functions that assist with manipulating strings. We will look at a couple of the common string functions first:

chomp(string)

The chomp function is designed primarily for use when reading from the keyboard, or from a file. It removes the trailing newline from a string, if it exists. Here is an example use:

```
$string = "the quick brown fox\n";
chomp($string);
print "String: $string";
```

An important thing to notice here is that nothing returned. That is because chomp manipulates $string directly. As a result, the print statement on the third line will not print any newline characters.

In Perl, it is not necessary to use parenthesis for internal functions. Functions you define yourself must use them, however. This can mean that you may see something like this:

```
chomp $string;
```

This will produce exactly the same result as using chomp($string).

Here is perhaps a more common example of how you could use chomp:

```
print "Enter your name: ";
$name = <STDIN>;
chomp $name;
print "Hello, $name\n";
```

$name is derived from a line of text, read from STDIN. We will cover exactly how this works later, but for now, just remember that using <STDIN> reads a line from the keyboard.

One issue with chomp() which is worth keeping in mind is that files generated in DOS/Windows do not just have a new line character to remove. Under these hosts, it is necessary to also remove any carriage return (\r) characters as well.

chop(string)

Where chomp makes a selective removal of a new line character at the end of a string, chop will remove the last character in the string – regardless of what the character is. This is a possible solution to removing the carriage return character from DOS/Windows files; however it does rely upon the file having both the newline and carriage return, otherwise the script will end up losing data.

One other difference with chop is that it will return the character that is chopped from the string.

The actual `chop` function could be used as follows:

```
print "Enter your name: ";
$name = <STDIN>;
$chr = chop $name;
if ($chr eq '\r') {
        print "Hello, $name\n";
}
```

This is the first time you have seen a conditional statement, so let's have a quick look at it. We are covering conditional statements in Perl next topic. Basically, they take the form of:

```
if (condition) {
        # Run this code if condition is true
}
```

Basically, they are a test to see if the particular condition is true. In this case, we are looking to see if the contents of $chr is the same as '\r'. If they are, then "Hello, $name" is printed, substituting $name for the name typed in on the keyboard.

substr(string, start, count)

Another way to manipulate strings is to grab a specific piece out of an existing string. This is useful if you have fixed length strings that are formatted in a specific manner. An example may be:

```
$str = "000:LC654:Something else";
print substr($str, 4, 5) . "\n";
```

This will extract out the string 'LC654'. Counting starts from 0, so if you want the first 2 characters of a string, you could use:

```
substr($string, 0, 2);
```

lc, uc, lcfirst, ucfirst

These functions are useful to convert strings to upper case or lower case. The functions `uc` and `lc` convert the entire string to upper case, while `lcfirst` and `ucfirst` only convert the first letter.

Here is an example of how you could use them:

```
$validname = "fred";
print "Enter a name: ";
$guess = <STDIN>;
chomp $guess;
if (uc($guess) eq uc($validname)) {
        print "Valid name\n";
}
```

Note that with Perl 5.8 and above, string functions such as `uc` and `lc` functions are aware of Unicode, so they will be able to convert to upper case and lower case for any Unicode character that has an upper-case or lower-case variant.

Exercise 2.3 – Working with strings

1. Write a Perl script ex-2.4.pl that reads a name from the keyboard (STDIN) and converts the first letter to upper case and the rest to lower case and prints "Hello, name. How are you today?" (Don't forget to chomp). (Hint: substr() is good for this)

2. Extend the script to ask for the persons' age. This time, let's look at using chop for manipulating the user input instead of chomp. Do you see any difference between the two in terms of how they are used?

3. Copy the following code to the file ex-2.5.pl:

```perl
#!/usr/bin/perl -w
$a = 5;
$a += 12;
print "$a\n";
$a++;
print "$a\n";
$a = 55 - $a;
print "$a\n";
$a = ($a * 6) / 2;
print "$a\n";
$a /= 9;
print "$a\n";
```

4. Run this code and observe its output. Attempt to match up statements with the output from the script.

Internally defined scalars

In addition, Perl defines a number of variables that you can use to help make things easier. One thing to note with these variables is that for most cases, the variable names are not intuitive, as they are set out this way to keep out of the way of your choice of variables when you are writing your script.

Here are a few examples:

Variable	Used for
$_	Default variable (often used by Perl when no arguments passed to an internal function call)
$< and $>	Real and effective user id.
$0	The name of the Perl script
$/	Perls input record separator (used when reading from files)
$!	Last error (used when interrogating what went wrong opening a file, etc.) Relates to the C "errno" value.
$$	Current process ID
$]	The version of Perl (ie. 5.008008)

Table 2 - Some internal Perl scalar variables

Summary

You will now have seen how Perl defines scalars, using mathematical functions and operators as well as some basic string manipulation. Scalar values are the basic unit of data within Perl. They can contain any single value. They can contain integers, floating point numbers, strings and much more. Some of the more complicated things that can be stored in a scalar will be covered later, but for now we are just looking to scalars to store those basic things.

In addition, we have looked at some basic internal Perl functions. If you are wanting to look for more functions that exist, have a look at the `perlfunc` manpage, which lists the available functions that apply to both scalars as well as other Perl data types. Remember that for type-less languages such as Perl that other data types means different means of storing data, such as arrays.

You should now be able to perform some basic string manipulation as well as some mathematical functions. While Perl provides a lot of these facilities internally, it is important to recognize that there are other code libraries that contain more advanced means of working with scalar values, which we will cover in later topics.

Review Questions

1. What function calls can you use for manipulating strings? Briefly, what do each of them do?

    _____

    _____

    _____

    _____

    _____

2. What is the difference between the chop and chomp functions?

    _____

    _____

    _____

    _____

    _____

Topic 3 – Basic Syntax

Overview

Syntax in Perl is largely a combination of C, Awk and Sed. While a few other language similarities can also be drawn, these are the major sources of inspiration for the structure of Perl.

Topic Objectives

By the end of this topic, you will:

- Be able to use conditional statements with Perl

- Have an understanding of files and file handles, including the differences between these concepts.

- Understand how IO redirection works within Perl.

Conditional statements – if

Any language must have the ability to make decisions in code. Perl offers a slightly different set than most in terms of how decisions can be made. The differences with Perl are made with the view of readability in mind, which is strange, as Perl often carries the label of an unreadable language.

The basic structure of a conditional statement in Perl looks like this:

```
if (condition) {
        Code to run if true
}
```

This is a fairly straightforward looking statement. In fact it looks near identical to C. The only difference between C and Perl in the basic layout of a conditional statement is that you must use the braces ({ and }) to denote the beginning and end of the block of code that the condition is tied to.

This brings us to the notion of a block of code. In Perl, code is executed in blocks such as those found within our conditional statement above. Whilst the script you write is notionally a single block of code, you nest blocks inside others to create your program. These blocks may have conditions assigned to them such as in the if statement above, or loops, or simply exist on their own.

Here is an example of an if statement in use:

```
if ($age >= 18) {
        print "You are allowed to vote\n";
}
```

In this example, we compare a scalar $age against the number 18. If $age if greater than or equal to 18, then the code inside the block is executed. If not, nothing is done.

For mathematical calculations, we use the standard mathematical symbols for less than, greater than and so forth. For string comparisons, we use a different notation, based on letters. This is so we are able to explain what type of comparison we are doing. Here is a table of different operators and their numerical and string equivalents.

Comparison	Numerical test	String test
Equals	==	eq
Not equal	!=	ne
Greater Than	>	gt
Less Than	<	lt
Greater than or equal	>=	ge
Less than or equal	<=	le

Table 3 - Numerical and String Comparison Operators

Consider the following example:

```
if ($name ne "Jason") {
        print "You are not Jason!\n"
}
```

This is an example of how you can write a string comparison using Perl. We are using ne in the place of != to inform Perl we want to perform a string comparison. Note that for string comparisons that whitespace, newlines and any other character is included in the comparison. As such, "Jason\n" does not equal "Jason". This is where functions such as chomp come in very handy.

There is another way to write this using another conditional statement – unless. It is the same as saying "If not true". Here is the same example written using unless:

```
unless ($name eq "Jason") {
        print "You are not Jason!\n";
}
```

As you can see, it shows the programmer that we are looking for $name to be "Jason", rather than checking to see if it is not.

In the above example, there is only one command being run. Perl allows a special case conditional statement to be run as follows:

```
print "You are not Jason!\n" unless ($name eq "Jason");
```

This may read closer to how the English language processes conditional statements in some cases.

Exercise 3.1 – Basic Conditional Statements

1. Write a script name ex-3.1.pl which asks a user for their name, and if their name is longer than 5 characters long print "That's a long name".

    (Hint, you can get the length of a string by using the length function call)

2. Copy the following code to ex-3.2.pl:

    ```perl
    #!/usr/bin/perl -w
    print "Enter your age: ";
    $age = <STDIN>;
    chomp $age;
    if ($age >= 18) {
        print "You are old enough to vote\n";
    }
    if ($age < 18) {
        print "You are not old enough to vote\n";
    }
    ```

3. Run the above code. Observe the output. Try it with a range of different values.

4. Run the above code again. This time type in the word "twelve". Can you explain what happens?

Defined Values

Consider this slightly more complex use for an `if` statement:

```
if (defined($name)) {
     print "Hello, $name\n";
}
```

In this example, we checked if the scalar $name is defined. In Perl, a scalar is *defined* if it has a value. As such, the function defined() returns true if the scalar is defined and false if it is not. It is possible to make a variable undefined using the undef function. See this example:

```
$foo = undef;
if (defined($foo)) {
     print "Foo is defined\n";
}
```

As you can guess, the words "Foo is defined" will never be printed, as $foo is set to an undefined value.

True and False Values

Every variable can be evaluated to be either true or false. Perl does not have a specific Boolean type (or any type along those lines) so the concept of true and false is applied to every scalar, array or hash. We will cover arrays and hashes later, but for scalars, *true* values are any string that has data in it, while *false* values are undefined and empty strings.

One of the advantages of this is that you can interrogate strings directly within if statements, making statements like this:

```
if ($condition) {
     print "Condition is $condition\n";
}
```

Note that this test is not the same as testing for a defined value – this is a Boolean test on the scalars content. While an undefined value will yield a false result, so will an empty string or the number 0.

Using elsif and else

Of course, it makes sense to allow the ability to string different conditionals together. Perl provides elsif and else to cover this.

First of all, let's look at else. The purpose of an else statement is to provide the ability to run code if the condition in the corresponding if statement is *false*. Here is an example:

```
if ($age >= 18) {
        print "You are old enough to vote";
} else {
        print "You are not old enough to vote\n";
}
```

Here we make the distinction that if $age is greater than or equal to 18, we print one thing, and if $age is not greater than or equal to 18, something different is printed. Again, as with if statements, there is a requirement to use braces for the block of code.

Another extension on if statements is the ability to use the elsif operator to concatenate conditions together. Consider this example:

```
if ($age > 18) {
        print "You are old enough to vote\n";
} else {
        if ($age == 18) {
                print "You are only just old enough to vote\n";
        } else {
                print "You are not old enough to vote\n";
        }
}
```

In this example, you have three possible outcomes ($age being greater than 18, less than 18 or equal to 18). A better way to write this would be:

```
if ($age > 18) {
        print "You are old enough to vote\n";
} elsif ($age == 18) {
        print "You are only just old enough to vote\n";
} else {
        print "You are not old enough to vote\n";
}
```

In this example, the first condition is tested, if it is true, the first block of code is executed. If not, the second condition is tested. And so on. There is no limit to the number of elsif statements you can put in an if statement. You also do not need to use an else.

Case statements

Case statements are statements where a single variable is tested against multiple values, and a different action is taken depending on the value of that one variable. Perl has traditionally not had a case statement in its language definition, until Perl 5.10[1].

The case statement keyword for Perl is given. Basically, it works on the idea that when given a certain expression, when a certain condition is met then code is executed. There is also a default code block if none of the conditions are met. The result from the expression in the given statement is assigned to $_ so that it can be interpreted.

Here is a simple example of how to use a case statement.

```perl
print "Enter a number: ";
my $number = <STDIN>;
chomp $number;

given ($number) { # Value contained in $number is assigned to $_
        when (1) {
                print "One\n";
        }
        when ($_ > 10) {
                print "Large\n";
        }
        default {
                print "Invalid number\n";
        }
}
```

It is also possible to put in a list of numbers using an array reference[2], regular expressions[3] and many other Perl features within the when test.

This feature is a relatively new addition to the Perl language, and as such not all installations of Perl will understand this yet. As a result you should only use this in places where you know that this code will be understood. It is possible to enforce this, and how to do this will be discussed in a later topic.

---

[1] Features new to Perl 5.10 won't work on older versions of the Perl interpreter. It may be safer to avoid using this feature if you don't have Perl 5.10 installed where you run your Perl scripts.

[2] See topic 4 for arrays and topic 8 for references.

[3] See topic 7 for regular expressions. It is possible to do a pattern match within a when clause.

Indenting code

Languages like Perl are reasonably flexible with how the code is written. Code like

```
if ($age >= 18) { print "You are old enough to vote\n"; }
```

is just as valid for the interpreter as this:

```
if ($age >= 18) {
        print "You are old enough to vote\n";
}
```

This style of code is often referred to as the Kernighan and Ritchie style, named after the inventors of the C language – mostly because it was the way they preferred to lay out their code. Most Perl code you will see will be formatted in this way, as it provides a simple, uncomplicated view of the code.

Another way to format Perl code could be like this:

```
if ($age >= 18)
{
        print "You are old enough to vote\n";
}
```

This is a common method of laying out code in languages like Java and C++. This method is legal in Perl, but is less common.

Exercise 3.2 – More Conditional Statements

1. Review this code – copy it into ex-3.3.pl and indent the code to make it more readable.

    ```
    #!/usr/bin/perl
    $a = 5; $b = 7; $c = 2;
    if ($a >= 6) { print "1\n"; }
    if ($b > 3)
    { print "2\n"; }
    unless ($c > 5) { print "3\n"; }
    else { print "4\n"; }
    ```

2. Run the code and observe the output.

3. Write a Perl script called ex-3.4.pl which asks the user to type in a color. If it's red, white or orange, say "What a pretty color", if it's green, black or purple say "*color* is not too bad" (replace the word *color* with the actual color), otherwise say "What color is that?" You should attempt to make full use of if, else and elsif in this script.

Handling Files

Files in Perl are managed through *file handles*. A file handle is an interface to read from or write to a file. Most of the time, you will open a file to either read a file, or write to it. It is possible to do both; however we will look at the simpler cases first.

Opening a file

Opening a file can be done using the open function call. Here is an example:

```
open (FH, "input.txt");
```

In this instance, we will open the file "input.txt" and assign it to the file handle FH. From here on, we don't need to refer to the actual filename; we do everything through this handle.

This example opens the file for reading only. We will have a look at writing files shortly.

To read data from the file, we use the file handle. Have a look at this example:

```
open(FH, "input.txt");
$data = <FH>;
print $data;
```

The line that reads "$data = <FH>;" reads a single line from the file handle. It will read up to and including the new line character (if it exists) or the end of the file. Essentially, this means that Perl can use new lines as record separators.

Perl has an internal variable that it uses for the input record separator: $/. Changing this value will change the behavior of *all* data read, not just for this file handle. Here is an example of how to set it:

```
$/ = "\0";
```

This will set the record separator to be the null character. (\0 is a special way of explicitly stating we want the null character). Setting this scalar to an undefined value (undef) will allow the whole file to be read into a single scalar value. For example:

```
undef $/;
```

Finally, to close the file, we use close () and pass it the file handle. For example:

```
close(FH);
```

Writing Files

By default, Perl will open a file for reading. To open a file for writing, we use the Unix-like:

```
open(FH, ">output.txt");
```

The difference here is the use of a > to inform Perl that the file is being written to. When a file is being written to in this fashion, *any pre-existing data in that file is destroyed.* If you don't want the pre-existing data to be destroyed, you have another option, to open the file in append mode. Here is an example of opening the file in append mode:

```
open(FH, ">>output.txt");
```

This will open the file and any new data is added to the end of the file. To actually write data out to the file, use print, but tell it which file handle to write to like this:

```
print FH "Stuff\n";
```

Note: **There is no comma between the file handle and the data you want to write!** This is a special case, as print normally requires a list of things to print to be passed to it. Using a comma here will result in a different thing happening. Instead, it will try and print the file handle out to the standard output, which is not what you are wanting here.

To confirm the file is opened successfully, you have a few options. First of all, you can use if:

```
if (open FH, $file) {
        # Perform file reads here
} else {
        print "Unable to read $file: $!\n";
        exit;
}
```

Note that we have made use of a new Perl internal variable: $!. This provides a text error for the last thing that went wrong – in this case, the file didn't open. It will print out a (hopefully) useful message like "Permission Denied" or "File not Found" in the even the file can't be opened, so that the user will know what needs to be fixed.

A shorter version is to use or to handle the second half. Review this example:

```
open FH, $file or die "Unable to read $file: $!\n";
```

Setting aside the function die for the moment, it's perhaps easiest to view this as 2 commands – the second command will be executed if the first one returns a false value. This works because of how Perl (and other languages) treat or conditions.

If the first value is true, then the condition for the overall statement is taken to be true, because the second value will not change the overall result of the condition. If the first statement is false, then the second statement needs to be executed to determine the overall result of the or statement.

Turning back to that use of die for a moment, its purpose is to provide an error message and then exit with an error return code. The use of the newline at the end is also significant – it suppresses location information for the error. If the new line is omitted, you will see something like:

```
Unable to read test.txt: Permission denied at ./script.pl line 34.
```

Using STDIN and STDOUT as file handles

We have already been making quite extensive use of these special file handles. STDIN is a file handle that means "the standard input". Similarly, STDOUT means "the standard output". These file handles typically refer to the normal means that the program receives input from, and output to the user. In the examples we have used so far, STDIN has come from the keyboard, while STDOUT is the terminal we are running the script on.

Under UNIX (and also possible under Windows, but with limitations) it is possible to redirect these file handles to come from (or go to) another location. This is all done from the UNIX command prompt – Perl does not actually know that this is occurring.

To do this, a script could be run as follows:

```
$ ./script.pl < input.txt
```

In this example, we are redirecting the contents of the file input.txt into STDIN. So in that case, any time we read from STDIN in the script script.pl, we are actually reading a line from input.txt.

Similarly, it is possible to redirect output that would be sent to STDOUT to a file. Refer to this example:

```
$ ./script.pl > output.txt
```

In this example, anything printed to STDOUT (using functions such as print, etc.) will be redirected to output.txt instead of the terminal.

Of course, it is possible to do both:

```
$ ./script.pl < input.txt > output.txt
```

The other possibility is to pass the output of one script into the input of a second script using a pipe. Consider this example:

```
$ ./script.pl > temp.txt
$ ./script2.pl < temp.txt
```

If you don't need to keep the copy of temp.txt, it is possible to do this using a pipe. Here is how it can be done:

```
$ ./script.pl | ./script2.pl
```

In the case of pipes, it is possible to do as many of these as you like, there is no limit. In addition, these do not have to be Perl scripts; you can run any command and pipe it into your script. For example:

```
$ ls -l /tmp | ./parse-tmp.pl
```

This will run the `ls -l` command on `/tmp` and forward the output into your script as if it was `STDIN`. A script that may handle this is as follows:

```
#!/usr/bin/perl -w
undef $/; # Read whole file into string...
$ls = <STDIN>; # Read in ls output.
# Processing of what to do with ls output would go here.
```

Summary

Most languages contain conditional statements. Perl actually contains slightly fewer than other languages. The conditional statements you have seen are slightly different to that of other languages, yet not by a large amount. Perl's handling of single line conditionals is unique, but it does aide code readability in certain circumstances.

Other things we have seen in this topic include how Perl uses any scalar to handle Boolean values. Perl ensures that every string has a Boolean value so that it makes testing strings considerably more flexible.

Finally, we covered file handling. You should now be able to open and close a file for both reading and writing. We have also covered reading from and writing to files.

Review Questions

1. For Perl, what constitutes a true and false value?

    _____

    _____

    _____

    _____

    _____

2. Which of the following is the correct way to open a file to append to the file?

    a. `open APP, "w+textfile";`

    b. `open APP, ">textfile";`

    c. `open APP ">>textfile";`

    d. `open APP, ">>textfile";`

Topic 4 – Loops, complex conditional statements

Overview

Loops form the core of any program, regardless of language. In Perl, a number of different types of loop controls exist. Some do not provide much of a difference, except to aide code readability (when used correctly, of course). In this topic we cover some of the basic loop structures that exist within Perl, such as `while` and `for` loops.

Topic Objectives

By the end of this topic, you will be able to:

- Understand and be able to apply some of the basic loop structures

- Use control statements within loops to affect how loops operate based on conditions

- Use some basic pragmas in Perl to define how aspects of the language are to be used

Loops overview

Loops in programming languages provide the ability to run a block of code multiple times. They may be run endlessly, or while a condition is met, or simply be run a set number of times, for example when iterating through a loop.

Perl offers a number of loop structures, such as while and until, do loops, for and foreach loops. Each of these has different uses. In this chapter, we will look at most of these loops (foreach we will reserve until we look into arrays more thoroughly in topic 5).

Loop structures – while and until

The most common form of loop are while loops. These are the standard form of loops that would be seen in most programming languages. The basic idea is that the loop will run through continually, for as long as the condition is met.

Consider this example:

```
$a = 0;
while ($a < 100) {
        print $a++ . "\n";
}
```

This example will print the numbers 0 through to 100, incrementing each time the print statement is run.

One possible use for while loops is to read through a file. For example:

```
if (open FH, "input.txt") {
        while ($line = <FH>) {
                print $line;
        }
} else {
        die "Unable to read $line: $!\n";
}
```

This script will read a file called input.txt and print it out to the screen. Note in Perl you will often not need to check if there is more data. Reading within a while loop like this provides you with an implicit end of file test. As soon as there is no more data to read from the file, the assignment statement will be false and the loop will exit.

The other form for a while loop is an until loop. This is the same as saying "while not". Consider this example:

```
while ($a != 0) {
        # Do something...
}
```

That can also be expressed as:

```
until ($a == 0) {
        # Do something...
}
```

As with the use of unless, the advantage of the until loop is primarily a readability issue. In the example, we run through the loop until $a is equal to 0, rather than running through the loop while $a is not 0.

An important thing to remember is that the loop will only execute if the loop condition is met *before* running the block. This means that if the condition is not true when the code is reached, it will not get executed. For example:

```
$a = 5;
while ($a > 10) {
        print "Never executed";
}
```

The code inside the block will never be executed.

Loop structures – do

One of the issues with `while` and `until` loops is that the condition is tested at the start of the loop, meaning the condition must be true for the loop to be executed even once.

Loops such as "do" loops get around this by testing the condition at the end of the loop, rather than the beginning. This means that the code block is executed first then the condition is tested. Consider this example:

```
do {
        print "Are you sure? (y/n) ";
        my $ok = <STDIN>;
        chomp $ok;
        $ok = lc($ok);
} while ($ok ne 'y' and $ok ne 'n');
```

As you can see, this allows a variable to be initialized and set with a real value before it is tested. Doing the equivalent code within a while loop would require something like this:

```
$ok = 'x';
while ($ok ne 'y' and $ok ne 'n') {
        print "Are you sure? (y/n) ";
        my $ok = <STDIN>;
        chomp $ok;
        $ok = lc($ok);
}
```

Loop structures – for

For loops are a slightly different arrangement to a while loop in that they are usually designed to run the loop a set number of times. The basic structure of the for loop looks like this:

```
for ( setup ; condition ; incrementor ) {
    code block
}
```

There are three parts to the for loop, each of them are optional. There is the *setup*, which is usually used to set up a counter variable or something similar, there is the *condition* which must be true – this is the same as for a while loop, and finally the *incrementor*. This is run each time through the loop and is generally expected to be something that gets the condition closer to being false – this way an infinite loop does not occur.

Consider the following example:

```
for ($i = 0; $i < 10; $i++) {
    print "$i\n";
}
```

This will run the loop code 10 times, incrementing $i each time.

One thing to note is that the for loop can be written in terms of a while loop quite easily. Here is the above code rewritten to use a while loop:

```
$i = 0;
while ($i < 10) {
    print "$i\n";
    $i++;
}
```

Loop control

Often, you will want the loop to restart upon certain conditions, or exit out once a particular condition has been met. For that, we are going to look at a couple of loop controls: next and last.

The loop control next will skip over this run of the loop and return control back to the loop condition. Consider the following example:

```
open PASSWD, "/etc/passwd";
while ($line = <PASSWD>) {
        next unless (substr($line,0,5) eq 'root:');
        print $line;
}
close PASSWD;
```

Reviewing what this does, it opens the file /etc/passwd then reads line by line. It checks if the first 5 characters match 'root:'. If they do not, then the loop is returned back to the top of the loop, another line is read and we try again. Whilst the condition we put above could also be written as:

```
if (substr($line,0,5) eq 'root:') {
        print $line;
}
```

There is also the possibility that we may want multiple conditions to continue, in which case embedding multiple conditional controls would make the code harder to read. Consider the following example:

```
open CFG, "config.dat";
while ($line = <CFG>) {
        chomp $line;
        next if ($line eq ""); # Skip blank lines in a file.
        next if (substr($line,0,1) eq '#'); # Remove lines that start with #.
        $config = $line;
}
close PASSWD;
```

This provides a simple way of ignoring pieces of information that we don't want to process from a file.

Another control is last. The last command can be used when we want to leave the loop altogether. This is possibly most useful when you are searching for information in a file. Consider this example:

```
open PASSWD, "/etc/passwd";
while ($line = <PASSWD>) {
        next unless (substr($line,0,5) eq 'root:');
        print $line;
        last; # We can now leave the loop as we have found the info we want.
}
close PASSWD;
```

In this example, we are leaving the loop as soon as we find the first entry that matches what we are looking for. If we didn't do this, we would read through every line of text in the file and possibly process it. Leaving the loop once we have what we want is a far more efficient way of programming this code.

Exercise 4.2 – For loops and controlling loops

1. Write a simple Perl script ex-4.3.pl which reads 10 set values from the keyboard and prints the average and maximum number entered.

2. Examine this piece of Perl code:

```perl
#!/usr/bin/perl -w
$numerator = 4;
$denominator = 1;
$neg = 1;
$pi = 0;
$maxiter = 10000; # Bigger number is more accurate, but slower

for ($num = 0; $num < $maxiter; $num++) {
    $pi += $neg * ($numerator/$denominator);
    $neg = 0 - $neg;
    $denominator += 2;
}
print "Pi = $pi";
```

3. Copy this code to ex-4.4.pl and run it. If you like, expand the value $maxiter to improve (but slow) the calculation.

Naming loops and blocks of code

Code blocks in Perl can be named directly. This provides certain advantages when dealing with loops, especially when there are quite a few loops that you are dealing with. It helps on two fronts. Firstly, it improves readability (especially if the names are useful and relevant) and secondly it helps from a programming level as it can allow you to address loops directly. Consider this example:

```
open FH, "file.dat";
while ($line = <FH>) {
        $ok = 0;
        open FH2, "file2.dat";
        while ($line2 = <FH>) {
                if ($line eq $line2) {
                        print "Match found for: $line\n";
                        $ok = 1;
                        last;
                }
        }
        close FH2;
        if ($ok == 0) {
                print "No match found for: $line\n";
        }
}
close FH;
```

At the high level, this script finds similarities between two files based on the contents of each line, and prints out some text if there is no common line in the second file.

Whilst there is nothing actually wrong with how this code is written (it will run just fine), here is a neater way to handle the same problem:

```
open FH, "file.dat";
LINE: while ($line = <FH>) {
        open FH2, "file2.dat";
        while ($line2 = <FH>) {
                if ($line eq $line2) {
                        print "Match found for: $line\n";
                        close FH2;
                        next LINE;
                }
        }
        close FH2;
        print "No match found for: $line\n";
}
close FH;
```

This example will skip to the next loop run for the loop named "LINE" whenever a match is found. Note we added in a line about closing FH2 before skipping to the next LINE. This is not strictly necessary, as Perls' garbage collector will deal with this for us, but it makes for nicer and more readable code, as it shows another programmer that we have finished with this file handle at this point.

Pragmas

Pragmas in any language are essentially notes to the compiler or interpreter that modify the behavior of code written in the language. In Perl, there are a number of pragmas defined for use. When they are defined, the keyword in the language is 'use'. We will cover the more commonly used pragmas here.

Use warnings

The use warnings pragma is perhaps one of the most useful. It doesn't actually change the language in any way, but it enables additional warnings that are normally suppressed. These warning are about things such as use of uninitialized values, reading on closed file handles and so forth. Here is an example:

```
#!/usr/bin/perl

$a = undef;
print "$a\n";
```

Whilst this is a trivial example, it shows the default behavior of when an uninitialized variable is used. In this case, a blank line will be printed. Now, if we put in the pragma use warnings at the top of the code:

```
#!/usr/bin/perl

use warnings;
$a = undef;
print "$a\n";
```

If we run the script now, we will get the following output:

```
Use of uninitialized value in concatenation (.) or string at script line 5
```

So the script will explain exactly what is going on and where it is happening.

The warnings pragma can also be enabled by using the –w switch to perl:

```
#!/usr/bin/perl -w
```

Use strict

The strict pragma enables controls on how variables are defined and used. There are three things that strict covers: Variable definitions, function references and symbolic references. We will cover the latter two when we discuss references in more detail. For now, lets focus on how strict changes variable use.

The first point is that variables can no longer be defined like this:

```
$a = 0;
```

You must now define a scope for the use of the variable. There are three scopes to choose from, and Perl provides this functionality regardless of the use of the strict pragma. The three scopes are "my", "our" and "local".

My

The my scope is the one most commonly used. It will define a variable to exist until the code block that the definition exists in is finished. It is often referred to as "lexically scoped". Here is an example piece of code showing the definition of a variable using my.

```
do {
        print "Enter your name: ";
        my $name = <STDIN>;
        chomp $name;
} while ($name ne "John");
print $name;
```

As soon as this do loop is concluded, the variable $name will no longer exist. Note that you don't have to clean it up yourself – Perl has a garbage collector that will ensure that variables such as this one are cleaned up when they are no longer required.

As a result, the above code will need a small change if we are to print the value out after the loop. It will have to look like this:

```
my $name;
do {
        print "Enter your name: ";
        $name = <STDIN>;
        chomp $name;
} while ($name ne "John");
print $name;
```

This way the variable $name is defined in the code block that we want to use it in.

It is possible to define multiple scalars (or arrays or hashes) with the one call to my. For example:

```
my ($a, $b, $c);
```

This will define 3 scalars ready for use in the current code block.

Our

The keyword `our` is used to define global variables – available to any part of the Perl script once they are defined. Functionally, they are not much different to using the `my` keyword at the top-level code block. Consider this example:

```
#!/usr/bin/perl
use strict;

our $basepath = "/tmp/foo";
open FH, "$basepath/config" or die "Unable to read $basepath/config: $!\n";
```

As soon as `$basepath` is defined, it is made available to all parts of the script. It is not, however, easily visible from within a Perl module (which are separate pieces of code anyway, so you probably wouldn't want that).

Local

The local keyword is the last of the variable definition types that we will cover. It is useful primarily as a means of having a temporary version of a variable within a code block. For example:

```
our $bar = 98;
my $foo = 89;
chomp $foo;
if ($foo > 10) {
        local $foo = ($foo * 3) + $bar;
        print $foo . "\n"; # prints "365"
}
print $foo; # Prints 89.
```

As you can probably see, its does not make the most intuitive code, so use it sparingly (and of course document it when you do).

"No"

No is the opposite of use – almost. For most pragmas, it will negate its use for the block of code that you are in. Consider this example:

```
#!/usr/bin/perl

use warnings;
$a = undef;
if (! $a) {
        no warnings;
        print "$a\n";
}
print "$a\n";
```

Then the warning will be printed out only for the second time that `$a` is printed.

Starting with Perl 5.10, it is also possible to use the 'no' keyword to enforce an older version of the interpreter (if a newer version would fail to run the script, for example. This can be done using the following:

```
no 5.10.0; # Require the interpreter to be older than 5.10.
```

Note: From now on, all examples and scripts in this book will use the strict and warnings pragmas. This is a good practice you should also adopt with your scripts as it will help reduce the number of errors in your code.

Summary

We have discussed some of the loop structures Perl can use. Whilst there is still the `foreach` loop which will be covered later, you now know how to use enough loops to write most programs. Loops such as `while` loops are useful general loops (as are until loops, which are the same as `while (! condition)`).

We have also covered the concept of variable scope, which will help to make your programs more robust by making better use of the Perl interpreter's garbage collection. Using variable scopes such as my and our provide valuable information to the interpreter (as well as the programmer) about how you intend to use that variable.

Finally, we covered pragmas, which are a way of dictating a particular behavior to the interpreter. The most common pragmas covered include warnings and strict mode, which are both very useful tools in writing robust Perl code.

Review Questions

1. What is the difference between a `while` and a `do ... while` loop?

    _____

    _____

    _____

    _____

    _____

2. What is the difference between a `while` and an `until` loop?

    _____

    _____

    _____

    _____

    _____

3. What is the benefit of using the `strict` pragma?

    _____

    _____

    _____

    _____

    _____

Topic 5 – Perl Arrays

Overview

Whilst single values are a good starting point for looking at data, Perl provides arrays as a means of listing out multiple values into an array. This topic covers how to define, use and manipulate Perl's internal array structures. We also revisit loops a little introducing loops that apply specifically to working with arrays.

Topic Objectives

At the end of this topic, you will be able to:

- Create and manipulate Perl arrays and lists

- Understand some of the loop structures and how they relate to arrays

Arrays

Perl defines an array as a list of scalar values all kept together. It can be used for a multitude of things, such as storing an entire file worth of data for later processing, or decoded records from a file.

This is perhaps a slightly different definition to most traditional languages. Whereas languages like C would traditionally set the size of an array, Perl places no such limitations. It will grow and shrink the array as needed.

Defining an array

Here is an example of how to define an array:

```
my @arr = (1, 2, 3, 4);
```

The first thing to note is the name. Arrays in Perl have the form @name. This is the name that you use when you are referring to the *whole array*. You do not use @arr when referring to a single element, as that single element is a scalar value, not an array.

To reference an element in the array, you use something like $arr[3]. The individual elements in an array are still *scalar* values, after all.

Here are a few examples of valid definitions for arrays:

```
# Empty array
my @array = ();

# Can be mixed data, numeric and string (and others not yet covered)
my @array2 = (1, 2, "Three");

# Join two arrays together (takes a COPY of the data in @array)
my @new = (@array, 4, 5, 6);
$array[0] = 5; # DOES NOT CHANGE @new!
```

Looking at these examples, the first defines an empty array with no data in it. The second definition gives an array with mixed data types. This is quite normal with Perl as we have already come to know. Since Perl makes little differentiation between

One interesting thing with arrays in Perl is that it some internal functions and operators behave differently if you are assigning the result to an array. Consider this:

```
open FH, "input.txt";
my $string = <FH>; # Reads a single line
close FH;

open FH, "input.txt";
my @strings = <FH>; # Reads the WHOLE FILE!
close FH;
```

The first example we have seen in previous dealings with reading from files; however this second read which may look similar, works differently. Because we are assigning to an array, all data in the file will be read into the array, split by new lines. So the first line of the file will be in array element $strings[0], the second line will be in $strings[1], and so on.

Manipulating arrays

Split and Join

Often, you will want to be able to encode an array into a string, or take a string and decode it out into an array. A common example of this would be when you want to use a comma-separated value file (CSV), which is a common format exported by programs such as Excel™, or from Unix files such as *passwd* files and so on.

The `split` function takes a string from a scalar and converts it into an array using a *delimiter*. This delimiter can be either another string or a regular expression, more on that concept later. For now, let's decode a CSV file we are reading from a file. Say for example, we want to sum up the numbers in column 3 (Remember, array index entries count from 0):

```
open CSV, "sales.csv" or die "Unable to read sales.csv: $!\n";
my $total = 0;
while ($line = <CSV>) {
        chomp $line;
        my @record = split(",", $line); # Decode the array
        $total += $record[2]; # Third entry is the one we want... Array
element 2
}
close CSV;
print "Total is $total\n";
```

In this code, we open the file, read in line by line and decode each line into an array. Note that Perl will automatically treat any numbers in the file as numbers, and non-numerical values as strings. No conversion is necessary. We can then total up the third field and print it out once the loop finishes.

The `join` function does the opposite. It takes an array or list of scalars and converts them into a single scalar string. The basic format for `join` is as follows:

```
my $string = join( delimiter, list );
```

The important thing to note here is that it is possible to add in arrays, scalars and other information which will be joined together into a single array. Here are a couple of examples:

```
$string = join(",", @list); # Simple - join an array only

$string = join(",", $name, @list); # More complex - a string and an array

$string = join(",", $name, @list, @list2); # Multiple arrays can be joined.
```

Push and Pop

One use for arrays is to use them for stacks and queues. Perl provides implementations of both of these concepts as internal functions. Let's start with a stack. There are two sets of functions that can work in this way, depending on which end of the array you want to work at.

In either case, the way you initialize an array for use as a stack or queue is the same as normal:

```
my @stack = ();
```

To place an item onto the stack:

```
push(@stack, $value);
```

This will place an entry into the array – at the end of the array. So if there are 5 elements in the array, using push will put the new value in as element number 6. This is straight forward so far. Let's take an element off the end again. This is done with pop.

```
my $value = pop(@stack);
```

This call will take the last entry in the array out of the array and return it. To highlight this, have a look at this code:

```
my @stack = (1, 2, 3, 4, 5);
print join(", ", @stack) . "\n";
push(@stack, 6);
print join(", ", @stack) . "\n";
$value = pop(@stack)
print join(", ", @stack) . "\n";
```

This will print out the following:

```
1, 2, 3, 4, 5
1, 2, 3, 4, 5, 6
1, 2, 3, 4, 5
```

And $value will contain '6'. The reason for this is that we are working at the end of the array.

Shift and Unshift

If we want to work at the start of the array instead, we can use shift and unshift. They are so-called, because they shift the values in the array. In the case of shift, the values are shifted out of the array, unshift places new values into the array at the start.

Consider the previous example, but done with shift/unshift:

```
my @stack = (1, 2, 3, 4, 5);
print join(", ", @stack) . "\n";
unshift(@stack, 6);
print join(", ", @stack) . "\n";
my $value = shift(@stack)
print join(", ", @stack) . "\n";
```

This example will print:

```
1, 2, 3, 4, 5
6, 1, 2, 3, 4, 5
1, 2, 3, 4, 5
```

Of course, $value will still have the value '6'. This is a stack arrangement; you will take off the value you just put on. However it's important to not here that the work is done on the left hand side of the array, and that has some consequences.

When you shift on a value as we did before, element 0 is shifted to the right, becoming element 1. Element 1 becomes element 2, and so forth. As a result, if you are using the array index values for anything, you should probably not be using shift, because as soon as you unshift something into the array, or shift something out of it, the association between indexes and values will have changed.

Reverse

The reverse function has a fairly predictable outcome; it returns the array, in reverse. Here is an example:

```
my @values = (1, 2, 3, 4, 5, 6);
@values = reverse(@values);
print join(", ", @values);
```

This example will print out the numbers 6, 5, 4, 3, 2, 1. One interesting part of reverse is that the result can be stored to a scalar value like this:

```
$values = reverse(@values);
```

The result will be a string of each of the values concatenated together in reverse. (I.e. "654321").

Grep and map

Quite often you will want to work on all values in an array at once. Functions like `grep` and `map` are useful when you want to either extract out specific information from an array, or make modifications to an array based on a particular set of code.

First, we will look at `grep`. The `grep` function works much the same way as the `grep` command in UNIX. It's not exactly the same, but is similar enough for most purposes. It provides a means to test each element of an array and include or exclude the element in the final result based on success of the test. Here is an example. Say we want to extract out all the positive numbers from the array:

```
my @list = (1, 45, -3, 2, -5, 9, 10, -9);
my @positive = grep { $_ > 0 } @list; # Note no comma!
```

Note that we have used a code block here to specify what condition we are looking for. This is one way grep (and map) uses to allow multiple statements to be used on each element. At the end of this, `@positive` will include a list of all 5 positive numbers in the array. Any element where that block of code returns a *true* value will be included in the array that is returned from the function call.

The other thing to note from this is the variable `$_`. This variable is an internal variable Perl uses for a number of things. In this case, `$_` is being used as a variable to denote what the current element is being tested against. In the above example, we are testing for each element to be above 0, hence the use of the test `$_ > 0`.

A common use for this function is to place a *regular expression* into the code block to extract out elements that match a pattern. We will cover regular expressions in topic 7.

Exercise 5.1 – Basic arrays

1. Write a script named ex-5.1.pl that reads a file line by line which contains data in comma separated values form.

    For every line, extract out the title (first field) and report the average and maximum value for each line. There are a variable number of readings (values) on each line. The data looks like this:

    ```
    Set 1, 5, 6, 7, 8, 8, 8, 32, 43
    ```

2. Place the following code into a file named ex-5.2.pl:

    ```
    #!/usr/bin/perl -w
    use strict;
    my @queue = (1, 4, 6, 3, 2, 6);
    print join(", ", @queue) . "\n";
    print pop(@queue) . "\n";
    print shift(@queue) . "\n";
    push(@queue, 9);
    unshift(@queue, 8);
    print join(", ", @queue) . "\n";
    ```

3. Run this code and observe the output. Pay particular attention to where elements are taken from with the `shift` and `pop` functions, and where they are placed with the `unshift` and `push` functions.

Other functions and variables

A few other functions that may come in handy are functions like `scalar`, which converts whatever is passed to it into a scalar format. When passed an array, it converts the array to a single number, which corresponds to the number of elements in the array.

```
my @array = (1, 9, 3, -2, 5, 3);
print scalar(@array); # Will print 6
```

Foreach loops

There is also a loop structure that is designed for going through each entry of an array. Loops using the `foreach` keyword will iterate through the loop once for each element in the array. The basic format of a foreach loop looks like this:

```
foreach iterator ( array ) {
      code block
}
```

The code block will be executed once for each element in the array or list. Each time through the loop, the variable listed as the iterator will contain each value in turn, until there are no more values to use. It will go through the loop sequentially, using element 0 first and going through to the end.

Here is a more complex example of using a `foreach` loop:

```
open FH, "application.conf" or die "Unable to open application.conf: $!\n";
# Strip out the lines that match a comment as we read from the file.
my @entries = grep { substr($_,0,1) ne '#' } <FH>;
foreach my $thisentry (@entries) {
      chomp $thisentry; # Remove newline
      next if ($thisentry eq ""); # Skip over blank lines.
      my @entry = split("=", $thisentry);
      warn "$entry[0] is set to $entry[1]\n";
}
```

In this example, we first grab out a list of entries from a file into `@entries`. We are using the `grep` function here to remove any lines that begin with a comment (any line that starts with '#'). We then step through each line and use the split command to grab out a key and value set separated by equals. Here is what a sample file may look like:

```
# This field does something really special
PATH=/bin:/usr/bin

MANPATH=/usr/share/man
```

Blank lines are handled using the line beginning with "`next if ...`" to ensure that we don't try and process those lines either.

Exercise 5.2 – Foreach loops

1. Take the script for ex-5.1.pl and replace the inner `while` loop with a `foreach` loop.

2. Take the code from the last example and place it into ex-5.3.pl. How could you get this code to remove lines with comments if the comment character isn't the first character? For example:

    ```
    # Comment 1...
        # Comment 2...
    VAR=1
    ```

Searching in arrays

A new feature in Perl 5.10 is to match against arrays[4]. It is possible to search through an array to find an entity, using the ~~ operator. For example:

```
if ($entity ~~ @array) {
        # Entity is found inside the array...
}
```

In this example, we are searching for the existence of the contents of `$entity` within the array `@array`. This is essentially the same as writing:

```
my $flag = 0;
foreach my $this (@array) {
        $flag = 1 if ($this eq $entity);
}
if ($flag) {
        ...
}
```

Since this is a new feature, it is advisable to require that this version of Perl is required to run the code. This can be done by using minimum version of Perl you require, using a *pragma*:

```
use 5.10.0;
```

Note that you should use three numbers in any version string. Anything else may cause Perl to misinterpret which version you actually require. Putting in '5.10' will cause Perl to interpret this as 5.100.0[5] (putting in '5.010' as a version will work, however).

If an earlier interpreter is used with your code now, an error such as the following would result:

```
Perl v5.10.0 required--this is only v5.8.8, stopped at script line 2.
```

---

[4] Note, this means that your code will ***only*** work on Perl 5.10 if you use this.

[5] This is because Perl interprets versions as strings, not numbers.

Sorting

Perl internally provides a reasonably efficient sorting method using the `sort` function. Essentially, this function takes a list of arguments and sorts them in either a pre-defined or programmer-defined fashion. Consider this example:

```
my @list = (1, 4, 7, 2, 4, -2, 67, 2);
@list = sort(@list);
print join(", ", @list) . "\n";
# prints -2, 1, 2, 3, 4, 4, 7, 67
```

Of course, the list can be inversely sorted using `reverse`:

```
my @reverselist = reverse(sort(@list));

@reverselist = reverse sort @list; # Remember, brackets not required...
```

Sorting does not have to be on numbers, sort will also sort a list of strings:

```
my @list = ("John", "Fred", "Stephen", "Jason", "Steve", "Sophia");
@list = sort(@list);
print join(", ", @list) . "\n";
# prints: Fred, Jason, John, Stephen, Steve, Sophia
```

The other thing that you can do with sorting is to provide your own method for sorting arrays. This is done by providing a code block that tests 2 sample values. The return value from the code block determines which value is bigger than the other. Here is a sample sorting an array in reverse numerical order.

```
my @list = (1, 4, 7, 2, 4, -2, 67, 2);
@sorted = sort { $b <=> $a } @list;
```

When using a code block to sort, each time the `sort` function needs to test if one is bigger than the other, it sets one value to be `$a`, the other to `$b` and then calls the code block. If the code block returns −1, then the value in `$a` is deemed to be larger. If 1 is returned, `$b` is bigger. Finally, if 0 is returned, the values are equal.

There are 2 special operators provided by Perl to assist with comparing values for sorts: <=> and `cmp`. The <=> function compares 2 numerical values and returns -1 if the left side is bigger, 1 if the right side is bigger and 0 if they are equal. The `cmp` function does the same, but for strings.

Here is an example of using the cmp function:

```perl
my @list = ("John", "Fred", "Stephen", "Jason", "Steve", "Sophia");
@list = sort { $b cmp $a } @list;
```

@ARGV and the command line

One array available internally in Perl is @ARGV array. This array contains all arguments passed on the command line (with the exception of the name of the actual command, which is stored in $0. Each argument is stored in a separate element of the array. By default, Perl does not attempt to make any sense of these arguments. Rather than that, it leaves you to determine how you want the command line arguments to be processed (if you want them processed at all)

Consider this code:

```perl
while (@ARGV) {
        my $this = shift(@ARGV);
        usage() if ($this eq '-h');
        setverbose(1) if ($this eq '-v');
        # Check for other arguments here...
}
```

This is a (very) simple way of checking for processing command line arguments by looking at @ARGV directly. In future chapters we will revisit this and expand on how command line options can be processed.

Exercise 5.3 – Sorting arrays and command line arguments

1. Sort the following list in descending alphabetical order using a line of Perl code:

   ```perl
   my @list = ("Jason", "George", "Graham", "Mark", "Malcolm",
       "Steve");
   ```

2. Write a simple script that prints out each command line argument separated by a newline character. Some sample output could be:

   ```
   % perl ex-5.4.pl This is a "simple test"
   This
   is
   a
   simple test
   ```

Summary

We have just covered the basic grouping of scalars, the array. As you have seen in the examples and practice exercises, arrays in Perl are a very flexible tool, given that the size of the array is not fixed like traditional languages such as C.

Arrays in Perl also have a few standard tools built into the language to make working with the language easier. You no longer need to write your own stacks or queues; Perl has these covered for you. Perl also has some reasonably efficient sorting functions in place with arrays, which further simplifies array management.

We also looked at the last loop type – the `foreach` loop. The `foreach` loop provides us with a very simple means of performing actions with a copy of each element in a loop.

Review Questions

1. How do you extend the size of an array in Perl?

   _____

   _____

   _____

   _____

   _____

2. What is the easiest way to reverse sort an array?

   _____

   _____

   _____

   _____

   _____

Topic 6 – Associative arrays (aka. Hashes)

Overview

Expanding on the discussion on arrays, this topic introduces hashes, an associative array. Hashes provide a means of associating a key with a value pair for easier retrieval. This topic will look at how to create, manage and manipulate hashes within Perl.

Topic Objectives

At the end of this topic, you will be able to:

- Create and manipulate Perl hashes

- Understand the circumstances where a hash is better than an array, and vice versa

What is a hash (or associative array)?

A hash is ultimately a set of keys that have specific values assigned to them. Where an array has an index to indicate where an element can be found, a hash allows a string or numerical value to take the place of the index. The advantage of this is that it will make locating values easier for the programmer, as they can have a more useful name associated with it.

A hash works on the idea that the key **must** be unique – this is the index that is to be used to find a specific value. Using two keys the same would make it impossible to specify exactly which element you are wanting. The value does not have to be unique, as there is no lookup done on the value.

A hash shares much in common with an array, it can be sorted (usually the list of keys is sorted), it can be reversed which swaps keys and values (**beware** that this can cause unpredictable loss of data if multiple values are identical).

Depending on how they are used, a hash may consume more system resources to use than an array, because the key has to be stored as well. There are circumstances where a hash is more efficient than an array; we will discuss those later in this topic.

Defining a hash

Here is the basic definition of a hash:

```
my %hash = ( key => value, key => value );
```

Hashes are identified by the % at the start of their names. Like an array, the % is used when referring to the hash as a whole. When referring to an individual element, the $ is still used. Here are some examples of defining a hash.

```
my %config = ( path => "/usr/bin:/usr/local/bin", manpath =>
"/usr/share/man" );
```

The first thing to note is that the key does not need to be in quotes – unless the key has spaces or other similar characters in it that may confuse the interpreter. Here is an example of why:

```
my %confuse = ( this is bad => "string value" );      # WRONG!

my %better  = ( "this is better" => "string value" ); # Correct
```

Enclosing keys in strings is often a better way when defining hashes to ensure that the exact string that you want is what is defined as the key, including any spaces or other characters.

When attempting to access an individual element in a hash, use the following notation:

```
print $hashname{keyname}
```

where keyname is located, place any string (quotes optional, but often easier to read if they are in place, especially with spaces, etc in the key name), a variable or a number. Note here that we use {} instead of [] when talking about hashes – this is so that the interpreter knows that you want to use %name instead of @name. Here are some examples of accessing hash elements.

```
$hash{valid} = 5;
$hash{'valid'} = 3;
$hash{"valid"} = 4;
```

Note that all 3 examples above are functionally identical. They will all set the same key (valid) to a value.

If we revisit the example of reading a configuration file in from the previous topic, some adjustments that make it more suitable to working with hashes could be:

```
# Create a hash to store configuration. Any settings defined here are
# default values that could be overwritten in the config file.
%config = ( datapath => "/var/datapath" );

open FH, "application.conf" or die "Unable to open application.conf: $!\n";
# Remove comment lines from
my @entries = grep { substr($_,0,1) ne '#' } <FH>;
foreach my $this (@entries) {
        chomp $this; # Remove newline
        next if ($this eq ""); # Skip over blank lines.
        my @thisentry = split("=", $this);
        $config{ $thisentry[0] } = $thisentry[1];
}
```

Let's take a look at the new changes that have been added in. The first is the definition of a new hash to store the configuration details in – instead of just printing them out. The key thing to note with that definition is that we are able to specify a bunch of values that we want to exist in our configuration – even if they aren't specified in the configuration file.

The second and perhaps less readable addition is to assign the keys and values into the hash. This is done with this line:

```
$config{ $entry[0] } = $config[1];
```

It's a slightly more complex assignment statement than we have covered previously. Take a closer look at it. The first thing to remember is that the previous split function call returned an array with (hopefully) 2 entries (There may be more than 2 if the value contains an = sign, more on that shortly).

The first element of our @entry array will contain the name of the configuration entry. The second value will contain the value we want it set to. So the *key* for this configuration entry will be stored in $entry[0], while the *value* will be stored in $entry[1]. So all we have to do is assign $entry[1] into the hash element with the key name in $entry[0], so we place "$entry[0]" in between the braces to indicate that is the name of the configuration entry we are changing.

Remember we were talking about the issue with having multiple = signs in the value? Consider this line of text for our configuration file:

```
EQUATION=Z=X+Y
```

In this case, we want the text "Z=X+Y" to be the value we are interested in, but since we are splitting the string on = signs, this is what we get (spaces have been added to emphasize this):

```
<-- 0 -->  < 1 >  < 2 >
EQUATION = Z      = X+Y
```

So when we assign the value $entry[1] to our configuration, only get "Z". The problem here is that our split doesn't know we only want to split on the first = sign, so it does it on all of them. The solution is to join them back together in our assignment statement:

```
$config{ $entry[0] } = join("=", @entry[1 .. $#config]);
```

Exercise 6.1 – Defining and using Hashes

1. Create a file named ex-6.1.pl and copy the following code into that file:

    ```perl
    #!/usr/bin/perl -w
    use strict;
    my %hash = ( key => 'value', 'key2' => 'value2',
        'command' => `ls -l` );
    print $hash{key} . "\n";
    $hash{key2} = 'value3';
    print $hash{key2} . "\n";
    ```

2. Run the code and observe the output.

3. Write a Perl script called ex-6.2.pl that reads a set of values in the form key=value and stores them into a hash. You could use the output of the UNIX command 'env' command as a source of information.

Functions applying to hashes

As with arrays, Perl provides a number of functions to aide in the use of hashes. Some of these are the same or very similar to the functions used with arrays – be careful as some of them do slightly different things when dealing with hashes. Most of these differences will be fairly easily understood, as they exist because there are differences in the concepts of an array and a hash.

Delete and undef

The `delete` function in Perl removes the existence of an element in either an array or a hash. In the case of hashes, the relationship between the key and value is removed, so that the key no longer exists.

Consider this example:

```perl
my %employees = ( sales => "John", support => "Jeff", marketing =>
"Richard");
delete($employees{'sales'}); # Removes relationship between "sales" and
"John".
```

The `undef` function is different. Undef will set the value of any scalar, array or hash to be undefined. The `undef` function will not remove the existence of the hash element, but will make the value contain an undefined value. It can be used on the hash as a whole to clean it out and remove all elements. For example:

```perl
# Create a hash to store configuration. Any settings defined here are
# default values that could be overwritten in the config file.
my %config = ( datapath => "/var/datapath" );

open FH, "application.conf" or die "Unable to open application.conf: $!\n";
# Remove comment lines from
@entries = grep { substr($_,0,1) ne '#' } <FH>;
foreach my $this (@entries) {
        chomp $this; # Remove newline
        next if ($this eq ""); # Skip over blank lines.
        my @thisentry = split("=", $this);
        if ($entry[0] eq "defaults" and $entry[1] eq "false") {
                undef(%config);
        }
        $config{ $thisentry[0] } = $thisentry[1];
}
```

We have modified the example above to manipulate the configuration import to allow the configuration file to blow away the default values. Now whilst it is somewhat less then useful, and this implementation does have its issues (which are left to the reader to discover), this change blanks out the contents of the configuration hash if it comes across an entry matching the required conditions.

Defined and exists

The `exists` function is used as a test to see if a key exists in a hash. It is also applicable to arrays, but is more useful in a hash environment.

Note that this test is only to see if the key is in the hash table – it does not test if there is a value associated with it at all. If you want to test the existence of a value, you will need to use `defined`. Here is an example usage for `exists`:

```perl
my %ages = ( John => 23, Jason => 25, Stuart => 39);
print "Enter a name: ";
my $name = <STDIN>;
chomp $name;
if (exists($ages{$name})) {
        print "I know who $name is. He is $ages{$name} years old.\n";
} else {
        print "I don't know who $name is.\n";
}
```

Now this test is somewhat problematic. If we had a key in the table for Richard, but didn't have a value in place for his age, you would get a response that looks something like this:

```
I know who Richard is. He is  years old.
```

For hashes, the `defined` function returns true if the hash element exists and has a value. It differs from exists in that it will actually test for the existence of a value as well as a key. An undefined value is not sufficient here.

```
if (exists($ages{$name})) {
        if (defined($ages{$name})) {
                print "I know who $name is. He is $ages{$name} years old.\n";
        } else {
                print "I know who $name is, but I don't know their age.\n";
        }
} else {
        print "I don't know who $name is.\n";
}
```

The key to remember here is that everything that is defined exists, but not everything that exists is defined.

Keys and values

These functions serve to provide a set of keys or values in the hash. They return an array of each key or value in no particular or pre-defined order.

One of the key uses for this is to set up iteration through a hash. Consider this example:

```
foreach my $key (keys %hash) {
     print "$key -> $hash{$key}\n";
}
```

This loop iterates through a hash and prints out the keys and corresponding values for the hash. The issue with this code is that it the order the keys are printed is not predictable. If you want to be able to put some order on the way keys are iterated, you will need to use `sort`. Here is how you could do it:

```
foreach my $key (sort keys %hash) {
     print "$key -> $hash{$key}\n";
}
```

Of course, you can always provide a function to `sort` to modify the behavior:

```
foreach my $key (sort {$hash{$a} cmp $hash{$b}} keys %hash) {
     print "$key -> $hash{$key}\n";
}
```

This example will sort the keys based on the contents of the value, rather than by the key itself. As you can see from this example, you have other information available when comparing values within a sort function.

Each

The `foreach` loop isn't the only way to iterate through a hash. One feature of arrays and hashes in Perl is that they include an internal pointer to a record – the idea being that the pointer can be used to keep track of where you are up to when working through an array. When the array is initialized, this pointer is set to point at the first element.

The only way to reset this pointer is to go through the whole hash or array (note that the `keys` and `values` functions also make use of this same pointer, so calling '`keys %hash`' will reset the pointer back to the beginning.

A common means of working through the hash in this manner is to use a while loop. Consider this example:

```
while ( my($key, $value) = each %config) {
        print "$key = $value\n";
}
```

This example will print out the contents of that hash.

There is one issue with using the `each` function – deleting or inserting elements. It is possible to either miss an element completely, or to run over the same element multiple times if you are inserting elements, so the general best practice here is not to alter the size of the hash you are iterating through until after you finish working through it. There is one small exception to this; it is safe to delete the key/value pair that was just returned by `each`. For example:

```
while ( my($key, $value) = each %hash) {
        delete $hash{$key} if (!defined($hash{$key}));
}
```

This example would safely clean out any elements in the hash that have undefined values.

System Defined Hashes

Of course, Perl does define some hashes that may be of assistance to you when working with Perl. Via the `%ENV` hash, it is possible to access (and manipulate) the running environment[6]. Whilst this is perhaps a more useful thing under a UNIX environment to Windows, it provides a handy way of communicating information to a child process. As an example, we may need to use a different location for the temporary files when installing a Solaris package. Here is an example of how this could be achieved:

```
$ENV{'TMPDIR'} = $SolarisTmpLocation;
system("pkgadd -d $SolarisPkgLoc " . join(" ", @SolarisPkgList));
```

In this case, we enforce a different location for the Solaris `pkgadd` command to use to store any temporary files.

---

[6] For information about environment variables, please visit http://en.wikipedia.org/wiki/Environment_variable

Another hash, also more useful in a UNIX environment is the use of signal handlers[7]. The %SIG hash is used to store information about what to do when specific UNIX signals are received. Handling signals in Perl uses features we haven't used before, but here is an example of how you could intercept a user pressing Control-C, which sends the INT interrupt to your Perl script:

```
$SIG{'INT'} =
        sub {
                print "Pressed Control-C!\n";
                exit;
        };
```

It is not necessary to understand exactly what is happening here at this point. We are defining a function that gets called each time an INT signal is called.

Exercise 6.2 – Advanced hash use

1. Given the following hash, create a script called ex-6.3.pl that prints out the names of any people over the age of 25:

    ```
    my %people = ( john => 23, jack => 37, jason => 23 );
    ```

2. Copy the following code to the file ex-6.4.pl and run it (pass in a text file on the command line):

    ```
    #!/usr/bin/perl -w
    use strict;
    my %words = ();
    open FILE, $ARGV[0] or die "Can't read $ARGV[0]: $!\n";
    while (my $line = <FILE>) {
        my @thisline = split(" ", $line);
        foreach my $thisword (@thisline) {
            if (defined($words{$thisword})) {
                $words{$thisword}++;
            } else {
                $words{$thisword} = 1;
            }
        }
    }
    foreach my $word (sort {$words{$b} <=> $words{$a}}
                                        keys %words) {
        print "$word: $words{$word}\n";
    }
    ```

3. Create a script called ex-6.4.pl and get it to print out (in alphabetical order) the currently defined environment variables and what value they are set to.

---

[7] For information about what signals are and what a signal handler is, please visit http://en.wikipedia.org/wiki/Signal_(computing)

Summary

We have now seen how hashes work in Perl. Hashes form an integral part of your data structures within Perl. As you will see in coming topics, hashes form an important part of producing more complex data structures. Creating hashes within hashes (or arrays) will allow us to create more complex data structures. Hashes also form an important part of the object oriented programming section later in this book.

Review Questions

1. What situations can you think of that you could use a Perl hash to assist you?

_____

_____

_____

_____

_____

2. What are the different ways you can print a key in a hash?

_____

_____

_____

_____

_____

Topic 7 – Regular Expressions

Overview

Regular expressions are a powerful, yet sometimes difficult to understand part of the Perl language. This topic explains the basics of regular expressions. We will also review the taint mode in Perl, and how regular expressions play a part in this security-based method.

Topic Objectives

At the end of this topic, you will be able to:

- Create basic regular expressions in Perl

- Be able to use regular expressions as a means to evaluate data, including validation

- Gain a basic understanding of *taint mode* in Perl, and how regular expressions play a part

Regular Expressions

Regular expressions are a means of performing pattern matching. Pattern matching is looking for specific patterns in a string of text. You aren't necessarily looking for a specific string, but you are matching against a general description of what the string should look like. These descriptions can be as specific or as vague as you require.

Regular expressions are a very powerful tool, as they are useful for data validation, extraction and many other tasks. Perl's "Taint mode"[8] relies heavily on regular expressions to validate data from an external source.

Perl has often been criticized as being a difficult to read language, and many people who say this point to regular expressions as proof of their claim. Whilst it is true that these can be hard to read[9], putting some thought into where and how they are used will ensure that they are used in places where it is appropriate, and where other methods may be more useful. Of course, documenting the regular expressions is also a good idea.

Here is an example of a standard regular expression. Here we are looking to see if a string contains the word "hello".

```
if ($string =~ /hello/) {
```

To dissect this, first of all, a regular expression test is denoted with the comparison operator =~. This means that a regular expression test will be performed on the string inside $string. The next point to make is that the regular expression is delineated by slashes. Anything between the slashes is part of the regular expression.

Finally we need to note that the result is sufficient for a test within an `if` statement (or `while` loop, or any other place where a condition is tested). This means that you could also perform tests like:

```
while ($string =~ /match/) { # While the string contains the word 'match'.
```

Of course it is also possible to place the contents of a scalar into a regular expression, for example:

```
if ($string =~ /$find/) {
```

Lets say for a moment that $find contains the string "Hello". This would now mean that we would look for the string "Hello" inside the $string. We can't use internal function calls inside the regular expression, however. This is easily worked around by storing the result into a scalar value before running the regular expression. For example:

```
my $check = substr($string,5,2);
if ($input =~ /$check/) {
    ...
```

---

[8] A method of ensuring that data coming from an external source is treated as unsafe.

[9] One such example posted on the internet is for validating email addresses correctly. See http://

Matching non-printable characters

Of course, not every character is easily represented within a regular expression. For example, new lines are referred to by the use of \n. Here is a table of some of the characters that can be matched[10]:

Character	Matches
\n	Newline
\t	Tab
\r	Carriage return
\f	Form feed
\N{NAME}	Named character (useful for matching with Unicode characters)
\x{hex}	Same as above, but matches based on a hex code for the character.

Table 4 – Non-printable characters

Finding multiple occurrences

The example of the search for a new line character also shows that we need to look for things that occur more than once, or things that may occur optionally, and so forth. Have a look at these regular expressions, which show the ways we can test for multiple occurrences of a string:

```
if ($string =~ /w*/) { # Zero or more w's

if ($string =~ /w+/) { # One or more w's

if ($string =~ /w?/) { # Optionally contain a single w. (ie. 0 or 1
occurences)
```

Perl will recognize the following quantifiers:

Quantifier	Matches
*	Match 0 or more times
+	Match 1 or more times
?	Match 0 or 1 time
{n}	Match n times
{n,}	Match n or more times
{n,m}	Match n times up to m times

Table 5 - Quantifiers available in regular expressions

---

[10] Refer to *perlre* manpage for a more comprehensive list

Brackets and special escaped characters

For the most part, matching within regular expressions is focused at a character level. As a result, it is possible to specify that a set of characters may exist at a particular location as part of our match.

This is done with the use of square brackets, and each possible entry is put inside the brackets. Consider this example:

```
$input =~ /[0123456789]+/;
```

This would match any number from 0 through 9. Any character inside those square brackets is matched. Remember that the intention here is to provide a description of what we are looking for. This means that we have to be able to be flexible with how we define what we are looking for. Using square brackets increases the flexibility that is available to us.

Of course, since there is always more than one way to do anything, Perl provides shorthand for the common cases of selecting ranges of numbers or letters. Instead of having to type out [0123456789] each time or worse still every letter of the alphabet, Perl will allow you to put in place [0-9] instead. This can be used for any range, so if you need octal numbers only, then you could use [0-7]. If you want all letters, both upper case and lower case, it is possible to place both within the brackets like this [A-Za-z].

There is one other special character to make note of here, and that is the use of '.'. In regular expressions, a '.' refers to any character. It won't matter if it's a printable or non-printable character, it will match the existence of a single character. If you have a match like this:

```
$string =~ /.*/;
```

It will match the entire string, because it matches 0 or more of any character.

Another requirement for regular expressions is the need to be able to group individual characters together. As an example, we may want to find 0 or more occurrences of a set of characters. If you make a regular expression like this:

```
$string =~ /word*/
```

The resulting regular expression will focus on the existence of "wor" followed by 0 or more occurrences of 'd'. If your intention was to find 0 or more occurrences of "word", then a slight change is required.

Grouping together a sequence requires the use of brackets. Using the brackets to join the characters together, we can then apply a quantifier to the group of characters as a whole:

```
$string =~ /(word)*/;
```

This will give us the ability to search for 0 or more occurrences of the word, but of course these would have to appear as something like "wordwordword" to be detected.

There is one other use for brackets – they save out the actual string that was matched. So for example if we have the following:

```
Print "Enter a positive number: ";
$input = <STDIN>;
# Match number, followed by optional . followed by more numbers
$input =~ /([0-9]+\.?[0-9]*)/;
```

After this code has been executed, $1 will match the number entered in by the user, if one was entered. It would extract the number out of whatever was typed, so any extra information could be discarded.

Because some matches like [0-9] occur quite commonly, Perl provides yet another shortened form using escaped characters. The most common of these are in the table below:

Character	Matches
\d	Digits (same as [0-9])
\D	Non-Digits (everything except [0-9]
\w	Word characters (same as [0-9A-Za-z_])
\W	Non-word characters (anything not in \w)
\b	Matches on the edge of a word.

Table 6 - Special matches

Exercise 7.1 – Basic Regular Expressions

1. Write a Perl script named ex-7.1.pl that reads a text file and extracts out any mobile phone number. For the purposes of this exercise, treat a mobile number as any 10 digit number that starts with '04'.

2. Write regular expressions that would find the following:

    a. The string "Good morning Vietnam!"

    b. Three question marks

    c. Split a comma separated values file into individual elements

3. Write a Perl script named ex-7.2.pl that takes an email address on the command line and verifies if it is correct. A correct email address contains the following:

    a. A sequence of letters or numbers, plus a dot, underscore or dash;

    b. The @ symbol, followed by;

    c. A valid domain name, which is one or more sets of characters followed by dots;

    d. Finally ending in either .com, .com.au or .org.au.

Search and Replace

One of the more powerful abilities within regular expressions is the ability to do a search and replace on a given string. The search takes the form of a regular expression, which matches the text to be replaced, and the second half of the expression provides what the text should be replaced by. Here is the basic structure of a search and replace:

```
$string =~ s/search/replace/;
```

If this code were to be executed, it would search through $string, find the first occurrence of "search" and replace it with "replace".

Recall this example from a previous topic:

```
$string =~ s/\r?\n$//;
```

In this example, we are looking for the existence of a carriage return and a new line, which form the new line in a Windows system. You should now know enough about regular expressions to take a guess at what this does. Have a think about it before reading on.

The example actually removes these new lines and carriage returns from the string. The empty replace section means that the match will be replaced by nothing, which means it will be removed.

Here are some more complex examples which use some of the other features of regular expressions:

```
$string =~ s/.*(\d+).*/$1/; # Chop out anything except the first set of
numbers

$string =~ s/\b(\w+)\b//; # Remove the first word from a string and store in
$1
```

Options to Regular Expressions

Sometimes additional modifiers are required to enable regular expressions to be a bit more flexible than they otherwise might be. An example of this is if you want to be able to match a string regardless of case. An example might be searching for a specific stock item:

```
print "Enter Stock ID: ";
my $stockid = <STDIN>;
chomp $stockid;
open STOCK, $stockfile or die "Can't read stock file: $!\n";
while (my $thisitem = <STOCK>) {
        # Stock item id is the first field.
        next unless ($thisitem =~ /^$stockid,/i);
        # Process stock item here...
}
close STOCK;
```

As you can see from this example, it will not matter if the user enters the stock item in the form of "item", "Item" or "ITEM". They will all be located using the case insensitive pattern match. Here is a table with most of the available modifiers.[11]

Modifier	Function
i	Makes the pattern match case insensitive
G	Makes the search and replace global. That is, find all occurrences of the match and replace them
S	Treat string as a single line. Matches newlines anywhere in the string
M	Treat string as multiple lines. The use of ^ and $ can happen multiple times within a single match.

Table 7 - Perl Regular Expression Modifiers

Exercise 7.2 – Advanced Regular Expressions

1. Write a Perl script named ex-7.3.pl that extracts any non-alphabetic characters out of a line of text. (For example, newlines, tabs, spaces, numbers, underscores, etc.)

2. Modify the email address script above (ex-7.2.pl) to search for the first domain name section and replace it with your company name.

---

[11] Refer to perlre manpage for the rest.

Greedy vs. Non-Greedy matching

By default, Perl will attempt to match as much as possible. This can present certain problems when performing a search and replace, or when you need to extract out information from a delimited record. For example, consider a CSV file like this:

```
1,Boots,Small,12,4.50
2,Shoes,Medium,42,8.20
```

Let's say we want to extract the product name (the second field) out with a regular expression. As a first effort, you would think that this would do the job:

```
$line =~ /,(.+),/;
```

Take a moment and have a look at what you think that it would match. Bear in mind that by default, Perl will try and match as much as possible. In this case, $1 would get the value "Boots,Small,12", which is the biggest match it can possibly make. Since we only want the section "Boots", we need to be able to tell the regular expression to be less greedy. To do this, we put a '?' inside the brackets after the '+'. For example:

```
$line =~ /,(.+?),/;
```

This will tell the regular expression to be less greedy when matching that particular part of the regular expression. What happens instead is that the smallest possible match will be made, which for the case of the strings we had above would mean that the string "Boots" would be matched. Of course, it can also be applied to any of the quantifiers already discussed, for example this would match 5 or more instances of any character:

```
$line =~ /(.{5,}?)/;
```

The important thing to remember here is that it does not actually change the definition of what is a successful match, only how greedy a particular part of the regular expression will actually be.

Of course, in the above example, we could be more specific in what we are matching by putting in \w instead of using '.', however this would mean that we would no longer match products with spaces in their names (For example it would not match "Ugg Boots".)

Taint Mode

Taint mode in Perl is a means of providing a more secure environment to run your script. It is meant as a way of hardening your programs by ensuring you validate any data that comes from an external source.

Essentially, what taint mode does is intercept any attempt to use tainted data anywhere that would result in it being visible externally to the program. Data directly input from an external source (for example STDIN, command line, external file, etc.) cannot be used to affect any external source (ie. written to a file, etc.)

As always, there are exceptions. The print and syswrite functions are not subject to taint checking.

Any internally generated data that comes into contact with so-called "tainted" data is then itself considered as tainted.

To enable taint mode in Perl, place the −T option on the command line (or # ! line), for example:

```
#!/usr/bin/perl -w -T
```

When taint mode is enabled on a script, it will add in a flag for each variable that indicates if the value is tainted or not. Any information from external sources is tainted and must be validated in order to be used externally.

In terms of detecting if a given value is tainted, there is no actual check implemented within the core Perl language. The documentation suggests the following code:

```
sub is_tainted {
      return ! eval { eval("#" . substr(join("", @_), 0, 0)); 1 };
}
```

It is left as an exercise for the reader to understand exactly how this code works. This function is included in the Scalar::Util perl library[12], which is included with Perl from version 5.8 onwards.

To "untaint" external data, it is necessary to push the data though a regular expression and extract the useful bits out of it. For example:

```
if ($string =~ /^(\d+)$/) {
      $string = $1; # $string will now be considered safe.
      warn "Data is OK!\n";
} else {
      die "Data is NOT OK\n";
}
```

This way, you have validated each and every piece of input before you use it, which is of course a good programming process to follow.

Exercise 7.3 – Using Taint Mode

1. Modify this script to work in with Taint checking. Ensure that the path both exists and is a valid path (ie. Starts with a '/'):

    ```
    #!/usr/bin/perl -wT
    use strict;
    print "Enter path: ";
    my $path = <STDIN>;
    system "/usr/bin/ls $path";
    ```

---

12 We will cover Perl libraries and modules in a later topic.

Summary

We have now covered regular expressions within Perl. Whilst there is the possibility that code written using Regular expressions can be the harder code to read within Perl. However the regular expressions in Perl are an incredibly powerful and flexible feature in the language.

Regular expressions have a multitude of uses. From manipulating strings of text to extracting useful data, they will come in handy in a large number of situations.

Review Questions

1. Write a of regular expression to change the string 'The quick brown fox' to 'The slow green turtle'

    _____

    _____

    _____

    _____

    _____

2. How can you assist future developers by making regular expressions more readable in your code?

    _____

    _____

    _____

    _____

    _____

Topic 8 – Functions and References in Perl

Overview

This topic covers two parts of the Perl language that make it possible to write larger and more complex code. Functions (also known as subroutines) allow the programmer to split out complex of repeated tasks into a separate piece of code, while references allow the programmer the ability to build more complex data structures. This topic will introduce the basics of both of these facilities.

Topic Objectives

At the end of this topic, you will be able to:

- Be able to create your own Perl functions

- Understand references, and the role they play within Perl

- Be able to create and manipulate references to scalar values, arrays, hashes and file handles.

References

A reference is a scalar value that holds a reference to the location of another value. The scalar itself holds no value; instead it holds information about the location of another scalar, array, hash, file handle, block of code/subroutine or other reference.

Creating References

References to data can be made in a few different ways. Firstly, they can be created as references to existing and defined variables. For example:

```
my $ref1 = \$scalar;       # Reference to a scalar value
my $ref2 = \@array;        # Reference to an array
my $ref3 = \%hash;         # Reference to a hash
my $ref4 = \*FILEHANDLE;   # Reference to a filehandle
```

This will make it possible to pass existing values as references through to functions[13].

References can also be defined to anonymous arrays and hashes. For example:

```
# This line defines an anonymous array and creates a reference to it
# in $arrayref
my $arrayref  = [ 1, 2, 3, 4, 5 ];

# This line defines an anonymous hash and creates a reference to it
# in $hashref
my $hashref = { key => $value, key2 => $value2 };
```

In the above examples, the anonymous array is made by enclosing the entries in the array within square brackets, while the anonymous hash is defined by using curly brackets.

Because references to anonymous hashes and arrays are stored in scalar values, it is possible to create some more complex data structures using these facilities. As a simple example, it is possible to create a two-dimensional array as follows:

```
My $TwoDArray = [ [1, 2, 3],
                  [4, 5, 6],
                  [7, 8, 9] ];
```

It is also possible to store hash references in arrays, array references in hashes, and so on.

---

[13] See later this topic for the function side of this.

Symbolic Referencing

Another form of referencing in Perl is known as "symbolic referencing". Basically, it means that you can use a string to reference the name of the scalar or other value you want to reference. For example:

```
$scalar = "hello";
$$scalar = 1;              # Same as $hello = 1;
${$scalar} = 2;            # Same as $hello = 2;
$scalar->[0] = 3           # Sets $hello[0];
```

At first glance, this may seem a little confusing. But if you stop and think about it for a moment, you will realize that this is both a very powerful and very dangerous function within the Perl language. Perl provides this mechanism as a means of trying to cope with programmers who try to use references that aren't actually references. You will recall that in most circumstances, the Perl interpreter will attempt to make the best of what you tell it. This is one of those situations, and it could either do what you intended, or it could do something quite weird.

You will note that in the above example, we didn't use my to define anything. The reason for this is that using the strict module forbids this practice. The reason is that it is very easy to accidentally use a symbolic reference when you intended to use a normal reference. Using the strict module removes the use of symbolic referencing to ensure that only the standard type of referencing can be used – which hopefully provides less confusion in your code.

Dereferencing

The golden rule of references in Perl is that they will always appear to be references. That is, they will not automatically dereference. Code such as this will not print out the value in the dereferenced scalar:

```
$a = 5;
$b = \$a;
print $b;
```

Instead, this code will print "SCALAR(0x1002f6ac)", which indicates that it is a reference to a scalar value. In order to dereference the scalar and have it print out the correct value, the following print statement would be required:

```
print $$b;
```

The "extra" $ at the start says that we are dereferencing a scalar. If it was dereferencing an array, we would use @. For hashes we would use %. Of course, for these it would only be true when dereferencing an array or hash *as a whole*. Here are some examples of dereferencing arrays and hashes:

```
my $aref = [ 1, 2, 3, 4, 5 ];
my $href = { key => 1, key2 => 2 };

print scalar(@$aref); # print the number of elements in the array reference
print join(", ", keys %$href); # prints the keys in the above hash
```

This is some alternative notation for saying the same thing:

```
print scalar(@{$aref}); # print the number of elements in the array
reference
print join(", ", keys %{$href}); # prints the keys in the above hash
```

This notation is sometimes useful to explain exactly what you are dereferencing. For example, take a look at the following:

```
print join(", ", keys %$href{'subhash'}
```

It is perhaps not obvious that the hash is actually contained inside the hash. This becomes even harder to follow when performing multiple levels of dereferencing (I.e. A hash within a hash within a hash).

The above examples are all fine if you want to dereference the array as a whole. If you want to reference a single element within an array or hash, it gets slightly more complicated. The key thing to remember is that it is the type of variable you are extracting that determines the use of $, @ or % for your dereference. Here is the syntax for dereferencing an array and hash elements:

```
print $$aref[0];
print $$href{'key'};
```

If you are dereferencing multiple levels, it becomes something like this:

```
print $$$aref[0][5];
```

There is an alternate (and in most cases more readable) notation for referencing elements from hashes and arrays, using the arrow operator ->. Here are some examples of dereferencing array and hash elements using the arrow notation:

```
print $aref->[0];
print $href->{'key'};

print $aref->[0]->[5];
```

Exercise 8.1 – Referencing arrays, hashes, etc.

1. Write the code required for generating a 9x9 2-dimensional array in Perl.

2. Write a script named ex-8.1.pl that reads in a single number into each element of that 9x9 array.

3. Check that each row and column contains the numbers 1 through 9 only once.

Functions and Subroutines in Perl

Functions were introduced into Perl for the same reason as any other language; to break up the code to make it both more manageable and to make it possible to abstract away more common tasks. Rather than have a large combination of conditional statements and loops that make a program far more complex than they need to be, you will now be able to simplify your programs by splitting them out into functions.

A function in Perl behaves a bit differently than most languages in that it does not provide a name for each variable passed through. Instead, it places everything (in the order it was passed) into an array called @_. This presents certain challenges, in that it makes passing arrays and hashes more difficult.

The basic structure of a Perl function looks like this:

```
sub functionname {
        print "Function should do something here...\n";
        return 1;
}
```

As you can see, the keyword for a function (or subroutine) is sub. When we want to leave the function, we can use return, optionally specifying a value for the function to return. In this case, the function will always return the number 1, which is a true value. This would mean that if the function was evaluated in a conditional or loop; we would get a true value returned.

In this particular example, we don't pass any values to this function; we would call it like this:

```
my $val = functionname();
```

Because every value in the function is stored in @_, we need a means to split this out into scalar values to make it more readable for us. One of the easiest and most common functions to assist with this is shift. As you recall, the shift function will take the first element out of the array. So we would want to do something like this:

```
my $value = shift @_;
```

Because @_ is considered to be the default array, we actually don't have to specify the name of the array to shift. It will figure that out for us. So in fact you can write this instead:

```
my $value = shift;
```

Of course, we always use my to define variables, especially in functions. This means that when the function finishes, the contents of the variables defined in the function are cleaned up and no longer visible, which ensures that everything is ready for the next time the function is called.

There is one issue with this style of function; if you pass an array to the function it must be the last entry passed. Consider this example:

```
sub func {
        my $value = shift;
        my @array = shift;
        my $empty = shift;
        ...
}
```

In the above example, the scalar $empty will never get a value, even if the function is called like this:

```
func($a, @array, $b);
```

Why? Because the call to the shift function will always return the array when the left side is an array such as @array. This means that there will be nothing left in @_ by the time we get to pulling out a value for $empty.

There are a couple of solutions, the first is to alter the order that things are passed to the array (if we only require a single array to be passed). This would mean that we first require $value, then $empty, then finally the remainder in the array @array. This is acceptable if we have a single array to manipulate. But what happens when you want to work with 2 arrays? Consider this example:

```
sub arraywork {
    ...
}

arraywork(@array1, @array2);
```

Have a think about this for a moment. How could you get this to work? If you know the lengths of the array are fixed, it is possible, but Perl allows arrays to grow and shrink. Still, if you know the size of the array will be fixed, you could do something like:

```
sub arraywork {
    my @array1 = @_[0..9];
    my @array2 = @_[10..19];
}
```

This allows you to specify a slice of the @_ array to split out your arrays to be used inside the function. This is a workaround that will run into big problems if the arrays aren't the length you request. Say for example your arrays are 9 elements long instead of 10; you will only have 18 elements instead of 20. Perl will not complain about this, it will simply extend the arrays you are using to the size you need and fill the blanks with undefined values. In addition to this, your first array will receive the first element meant to go to the second array.

The other means you have is to pass by reference.

Passing references to subroutines

Passing references instead of real values is nothing new; most languages provide a feature to do this. Perl's method is not much different to other languages. The only thing to watch when passing references through functions is to remember that they are references. Since Perl doesn't do any translation on references. All that is actually passed into the subroutine is a single scalar value.

This method allows the program to know all the important details about how long the array actually is. Consider this example:

```
my @array = (1, 2, 3);
my @array2 = (4, 5, 6);

function(\@array, \@array2);

sub function {
    my $arr = shift;
    my $arr2 = shift;
    my @combined = ();
    my $count = 0;
    while ($count < scalar(@{$arr})) {
        $combined[$count] = $arr->[$count] + $arr2->[$count];
        $count++;
    }
    return \@combined;
}
```

As you can see from this example, the two arrays are kept quite separate. We don't have to provide information about how long arrays are going to be. Something to keep in mind here is that since we are passing by reference there is only one copy of the data, so any changes to this data will result in changes outside of the function the data was passed to. If you want to manipulate your own copy of an array passed by reference, you will need to take a copy of the data first. For example:

```
sub manipulate {
    my $aref = shift;
    my @array = @{$aref}; # Copy the array
    $array[0] = "Something different";
    ...
```

Taking a copy of an array (or hash) is a fairly simple thing to do, but it may not be a smart thing to do if the array contains a large volume of data, as it may take a while to complete, and it may consume a large amount of system resources to have multiple copies of an array. In those circumstances, it may be a wiser choice to keep only a single copy of the array and pass a reference to the array around when you need to modify the array.

Exercise 8.2 – Building Functions

1. Taking the script ex-8.1.pl, extract the validity check into a subroutine named
    sudoku_check that takes a reference to a 9x9 array and returns 1 if it is valid and undef
    or 0 if it is invalid.

2. Write a script ex-8.2.pl that contains a function that calculates pi (for the code to calculate pi,
    see exercise 4.2. Use this function to calculate the area of a circle (input for diameter of the
    circle can be either on the command line or taken from STDIN.

Anonymous subroutines

Anonymous subroutines are the result of combining the concept of references with the concept of subroutines or code blocks. Their primary use is as a means of providing a facility to do call-back routines within libraries, often graphics libraries such as Tk.

The simpler use for anonymous functions is to look at how Perl works with signal handlers within UNIX. UNIX provides a signal handling system to allow programs (or the operating system) the ability to send basic messages to a running program. It takes the name signaling from the concept of signals passed between ships or to pilots of airplanes. The idea is not to convey large amounts of information, but to ensure that when the signal is seen by the intended recipient, that it will do something appropriate.

Perl has a pre-defined hash %SIG to handle signals. Each signal that the operating system can send has an element in the hash. For example, there is a signal INT has an element $SIG{'INT'}. Whenever that signal is received by a process (in the case of INT, it's usually when someone presses Control-C on the terminal where the application is running), Perl will look in the %SIG array for an anonymous subroutine. If there is a code reference, it is executed. If not, then Perl will terminate the process (which is what processes are expected to do if they do not have a specific signal handler). So for example:

```
$SIG{'INT'} = sub {
    print "Someone pressed Control+C\n";
}
```

In this case, if someone pressed Control + C (which sends INT to the process) instead of the process terminating (which is what would normally happen) this code is executed instead. So instead of terminating, it will print some text to the screen and continue.

Special code blocks

In addition to subroutines, Perl provides an additional facility for calling code at particular times. These are used by the Perl interpreter to execute code at either the beginning or end of your script.

These are implemented in Perl as special code blocks named BEGIN or END. The BEGIN block of code will be executed before the rest of the code is compiled or run by the interpreter; while the END block will be run after you exit from your script.

The most common use for a BEGIN block of code is to set up an environment for your script to run in. For example, perhaps certain files need to exist. Here is an example:

```
BEGIN {
        if (-e "/tmp/tmpfile.$$") {
                # Possible security flaw of someone trying to mess with our
script.
                # Either that or we forgot to clean it up last time...
                unlink "/tmp/tmpfile.$$";
        }
}
```

In this example, we are testing before the code is compiled to see if the script was cleaned up after the last run. It's also possible that if we aren't careful that someone could do something nasty with temporary data. One example of this is to create a symlink in /tmp to another location. When we open to write, we open the symbolic link instead and that puts our temporary data somewhere else. This code ensures that if there is anything in the way of what we are trying to do that it is removed before we start.

END blocks can be useful to ensure that files or other resources are cleaned up once the script exits. For example, let's have a script that can create a temporary file in /tmp. An END block ensures that it has been cleaned out:

```
END {
        unlink "/tmp/tmpfile.$$" if (-e "/tmp/tmpfile.$$");
}
```

It is possible to define multiple blocks all with the name BEGIN or END. BEGIN blocks will be executed in the order they are defined, while END blocks will be executed in reverse order. So in this example:

```
BEGIN { print "1\n"; }
BEGIN { print "2\n"; }
BEGIN { print "3\n"; }
END { print "1\n"; }
END { print "2\n"; }
END { print "3\n"; }
```

This script will print:

```
1
2
3
3
2
1
```

It does not matter if the BEGIN and END blocks are interleaved in any way, they will be found by the interpreter in the order they are defined.

Summary

References in Perl provide the mechanism to make larger and more complex data structures within Perl. Multi-dimensioned arrays become possible, as well as mixing arrays and hashes and link them with both data and code.

The way that references have been implemented in Perl also means that call backs and other similar code references are easy to implement, you will recall our discussions about %SIG in a previous topic.

We have also covered subroutines, which we will go into more depth in the next topic when we discuss packages and Object Oriented programming. Subroutines behave quite differently in Perl compared to many other languages, so it is worth making sure you understand these differences.

Review Questions

1. Write some code that dereferences an array element.

   _____

   _____

   _____

   _____

   _____

2. Give an example of a more complex data structure that could be achieved using references.

   _____

   _____

   _____

   _____

   _____

Topic 9 – OO Perl – packages and modules

Overview

This topic explores the basics of creating packages in Perl. In addition, we will look at how Perl has a slightly different view of Object Oriented programming when compared to most other languages. We will create a simple class and write a script that uses that class.

Topic Objectives

At the end of this topic, you will be able to:

- Create basic Perl packages

- Understand how Perl uses packages to implement Object-Oriented techniques

- Create simple Object Oriented classes in Perl

Packages

Perl was originally designed as a functional language in the late 1980's, when object oriented programming was less common. As a result, object oriented functionality was grafted onto the language, as it was for many other languages, such as C (the result being a different language altogether, C++).

Perl decided to provide a fairly basic mechanism for object oriented programming, the package. A package is not strictly speaking an object oriented programming language construct; it is merely a way of having a code library. And it is in this capacity that we will look at it first. We will expand it to become a more object oriented facility later.

Essentially, what we will use Perl for initially is a way of holding a common set of functions. These functions are usually loosely related, and do not necessarily work on the same set of data. For example, you could create a package that calculates the area of different geometrical shapes. There is no common data, but the functions in the package will work on similar data.

Perl provides packages via a framework of Perl *modules*. These modules are typically a separate file which is named in the same way as the name of the package, but with a .pm extension. For example, if you were to write a package named 'Test', the package file would be called 'Test.pm'. It is possible to have a directory hierarchy of modules, for which the Perl module name is separated by 2 colons, for example the Perl module Net::FTP would have a perl module file named Net/FTP.pm

These modules do not need to live with the script. The Perl interpreter allows the use of a search path, called the include path. This path contains a list of directories to search when looking for an appropriate module.

Perl provides a number of packages built into the interpreter; many more are available from CPAN[14]. We will cover those later.

Let's look at writing ourselves a package. The example before of a library of mathematical functions to calculate area of objects is a simple one to start with. If we call the module 'Area', and create the file 'Area.pm' (under UNIX, the case of the filename is significant, but not if done under Windows). At the top of the file, we put the line:

```
package Area;
```

This tells us that we are using the Area namespace. Essentially, the only difference between a Perl package and your normal script is that we are using a separate namespace. The default namespace used by your Perl scripts is called 'main'.

From here, we can write whatever we need for our package. So let's put in a function for calculating the area of a square:

```
sub square {
    my $side = shift;
    return $side * $side;
}
```

This is nothing new. Now let's go and place a function for calculating the area of a circle:

```
sub circle {
    my $diameter = shift;
    return 3.14159 * $diameter;
}
```

---

[14] Comprehensive Perl Archive Network. Available at http://www.cpan.org/

Now we get to an interesting point with packages – they don't just contain functions like regular classes. It is acceptable to put in code outside the functions. For example, lets define $pi as a global variable, rather than have to type its value into every function that uses it. We could write it as follows:

```
package Area;

our $pi = 3.14159;
```

The package line is just there as a guide to where you could place the new code. You do not need to write it a second time. Now that we have changed that, we can now modify our circle function to look more like this:

```
sub circle {
      my $diameter = shift;
      return $pi * $diameter;
}
```

Finally, at the end of the module, you need to place the following:

```
1;
```

The reasons for this are largely historical, but packages need to return a "true" value, so that they can be correctly imported into your script. Placing this small piece of code at the end of your package is a simple way of ensuring that the package returns a true value. It is of no real use, but it stops the interpreter from complaining.

Importing and using your package

OK. Now we have a package, its time to show how to use it. Perl provides 2 commands for including Perl modules and packages. The first is require. Essentially, it will include the package file containing your module into your program as if the contents of the file were put directly in place.

It is possible to have Perl run other scripts inline with this method, for example:

```
if ($exec) {
      require 'part-b.pl';
}
```

This would mean that if $exec is true, that the contents of part-b.pl will be executed. The script in part-b.pl will have access to the variables defined in the original script, and can modify them as it sees fit. Note that requiring a file will only allow the file to be included once.

One other characteristic of require is that it will do any loading at runtime, which means that the code must be checked at the time it is loaded. If you want to have the module checked and compiled before anything is run, then you will need to use the use keyword.

For most applications, there is little difference between require and use, however the use keyword is more commonly used because of the extra things that it can do. It is essentially the same as require, but instead of compiling your code at runtime, use will compile it with the rest of your program, and that it imports symbols from that package into the package or script that called it.

As a general rule, the use keyword is a preferable option unless you have a specific requirement to use require. This is especially true of modules you haven't written yourself.

Here is an example of using the use keyword:

```
#!/usr/bin/perl -w
use strict;
use Area;
```

Now that we have a module and we have included it into our script, we need to be able to call functions from it. The way it is called will be slightly different to what you have seen so far, as we need to explain to our Perl script that we want to call a function from the package.

To do this, we put the package name first followed by 2 colons followed by the function we want to call. So say we wanted to find out the area of a square with a side length of 5 we would call the area function as follows:

```
print "The area of the square is " . Area::square(5) . "\n";
```

This would print out something like:

```
The area of the square is 25
```

Exercise 9.1 – Basic packages

1. Write a package called 'Volume' that implements calculates the volume for a number of different shapes (such as cube, rectangle, sphere and so on).

2. Write a script ex-9.1.pl that makes use of this module and calls each of the functions that you have defined.

@INC included directories.

When you include a module using use, Perl will search through a list of directories that contain Perl libraries. This list is similar to how the LD_LIBRARY_PATH environment works in Solaris. The process is that when the program needs to load a new library, it looks at the first directory in @INC for the module. If it isn't there, it goes to the second entry, and so on. If it goes through all the entries in @INC and still can't find the module specified, an error will be raised.

While the initial list is defined when Perl is compiled, it is possible to manipulate this list in multiple ways, depending on what your requirements are. You can modify the list either via an environment variable, which will apply to all Perl scripts you run, or you can do it on a per-module level at compile time or at run time.

To enable a system wide directory for locating Perl modules, you can define the PERLLIB environment variable. This contains a list of directories separated by a colon. These directories will be searched for Perl modules alongside the standard ones defined by Perl. Note that this is not set in your Perl script itself. This gets placed in the login environment for the user that will run the script:

```
setenv PERLLIB /path            # C-Shell style notation

PERLLIB=/path; export PERLLIB   # Bourne Shell style notation
```

This method is useful if you have a number of scripts that use the same extra directory for modules, and you have a level of control over the users' environment. Where that is not the case, you may want to put something in the script which tells it about where to look.

On the Perl command line, there is the -I flag, much like the one used in most C compilers. It will include another directory at compile time. You specify the path to -I as follows:

```
#!/usr/bin/perl -w -I/path
```

Multiple paths would mean you would use multiple −I flags. This is not the preferred method for including directories in to library paths. The best method to modify @INC on a per-script basis is to use the lib module. This pragma (after all, it modifies Perl's behavior) will add a directory to the path at compile time. Here is an example of how to use this pragma:

```
#!/usr/bin/perl -w
use lib '/path';
use Area;
```

This will include /path into the list of directories to check. One advantage is that the list can be modified programmatically, for example:

```
use lib "$ENV{HOME}/perllib";
```

This would include the perllib directory out of the users' home directory. This is primarily useful if you don't know where the libraries will end up in the file system.

Object Oriented Programming in Perl

Perl wasn't originally designed as an object oriented programming language. Like most scripting languages developed before the mid 90's, it was originally designed in a structured programming style. One of the benefits of modular code in Perl is the ability for the language to adopt some object oriented techniques.

This section is not intended to give you coverage of what object oriented programming is. We will leave that as a task for you to research on your own.[15] Rather we will be covering more of how Perl views object oriented concepts, which is a view that is somewhat different to what you may have seen in other languages.

Perl does not implement all of the concepts of an object oriented language. For example, there is no such thing as a private function or variable. Whilst this is perhaps unfortunate, it does keep in the style of Perl's desire to be friendlier to the programmer, even if it can lead to their own downfall. Certain circles[16] view this along the lines of you not entering someone's house because you aren't invited, not because the owner has a loaded shotgun.

So it is important when programming in Perl to keep in mind that someone may not use your code the way you had intended. This is true of any language; however Perl programmers have to be more mindful about this than most due to the open nature of Perl packages.

Roughly speaking, a class translates to a package in Perl's view of the world. Not all packages are classes, but all classes are packages.

---

[15] Some starting points could be:

[16] Such as the Programming Perl (Camel) book

A package that wishes to act as a class must have a few basics. Perl keeps these to a minimum and most of these features are optional. The first thing that any class requires is a constructor, a method that creates an object of a class. Normally that function is named something specific; however Perl does not put any particular requirements on the existence of the constructor. They are optional. Should you need a constructor there is no requirement to call it anything specific, although there is a convention followed that it be called `new`. This is not always followed, as it depends on the class as to what is a more appropriate name. The only requirement for a constructor is that it returns an object for the class. This is done using the `bless` function call. Here is a very simple example of a constructor:

```
sub new {
        # The most common way of creating a class is to use a hash reference.
        # These allow easy creation of a complex data structure that is easily
        # passed around.
        my $obj = {};
        bless $obj;
        return $obj;
}
```

As you can see from this example, there is a basic hash reference created, blessed then returned to the calling program for later use. It is common (but not a requirement) to use a hash reference for the blessed entity. The reason being is that it is then easy to create attributes for the object.

Most classes in Perl don't require destructors, as the garbage collector does most of the required work. For the times where you do need a destructor, define a function named `DESTROY` to perform this work. This function never need be called directly; the garbage collector will call it before it cleans up the memory used by the object.

Let's create a basic class that implements a prioritized queue. Its first in, first out, but entries can be allocated a priority to ensure they are dealt with faster. We begin by creating a file named "PriorityQueue.pm", which holds our class. In it, we put in the package name:

```
package PriorityQueue;
```

Now, for the sake of simplicity, we will skip over the additional commenting and documentation that you would normally place in these modules. We will next import some modules we need and create a couple of class variables:

```
use strict;
our $VERSION = 0.1;
our $DEFPRIORITY = 5;
```

Defining a scalar `$VERSION` like this allows us to both keep track of the version requirements, as well as allow a `require` statement to demand a specific version of our class if necessary. The `$DEFPRIORITY` variable is used later for assigning a default priority to any entry that doesn't pass one in the push function. Now we create the constructor:

```
sub new {
    my $self = {
                'queue' => []
               };
    return bless $self;
}
```

Now we need a function to push something onto the new queue, with an optional priority. If a priority isn't assigned then we give it the default.

```perl
sub push {
    my $self = shift;
    my $value = shift;
    my $priority = shift;
    # Give the default when none has been given.
    $priority = $DEFPRIORITY if (! Defined($priority));
    push @{$self->{'queue'}}, [ $value, $priority ];
    return 1; # SUCCESS
}
```

Functions that are meant to be used as object methods will have the object passed to them as the first element of @_. This means that you will need to remember to pull it away to a scalar before you start working on the rest of the function. There is a convention to use the scalar $self for this, but it is not strictly necessary.

Now we have that, we need a function to pop out the entry with the highest priority. For that, we will choose the one with the largest number.

```perl
sub pop {
    my $self = shift;
    # Get us a priority sorted version of the array.
    my @array = sort { $a->[1] <=> $b->[1] } @{$self->{'queue'}};
    # Grab the one we want.
    my $entry = pop @array;
    # Replace the array in our object with the new array.
    $self->{'queue'} = \@array;
    return $entry->[0];
}
```

Finally, we need to put in the end of the package:

```perl
1;
```

And we are done. To use this, we will need to create a Perl script that uses this module and creates a new object. Here is the start of the script:

```perl
#!/usr/bin/perl -w
use strict;
use PriorityQueue;
```

Now when we create a variable of an object, there are two notations that can be used. Here is the more commonly used one:

```perl
my $queue = new PriorityQueue;
```

This is the other method that is also correct, but less commonly used.

```perl
my $queue = PriorityQueue->new();
```

The difference is that the second one is explicitly calling the constructor, where as the first method calls the same method, but in a different way. There are no differences here. If data needed to be passed to the constructor, then it's possible to do it with both.

Now that we have an object, let's put in some basic values:

```
$queue->push(5);
$queue->push(2, 3);
$queue->push(7, 8);
$queue->push(2, 9);
$queue->push(1, 2);
$queue->push(9, 6);
$queue->push(7, 7);
$queue->push(2, 12);
$queue->push(10);
```

The first thing to note here is that we have used a slightly different notation to call the function. This is the method used when calling an object method, as it passes the object through as the first argument. Since it does this, it is possible to call it like this:

```
PriorityQueue::push($queue, 1, 2);
```

But this is rarely done, as it disguises the fact that the focus of the call is on that particular queue.

Now we have this done, we can pop off the highest priority element. We do that with this function call:

```
my $item = $queue->pop();
```

This will pop off the value 2, as it has the highest priority in the queue (12).

Exercise 9.2 – Object Oriented Perl

1. Write a Perl class named 'BookLine', which will form the basis of a book stores stock collection. Build a constructor method called `new` that will create a new line of books and will be called with 4 arguments like this:

```
my $book = new BookLine("Title", "Author", 9.95, 3);
```

2. Define the following methods: `buy`, `sell`, `price` and `stock`. They will be called like this:

```
$book->buy(5); # Add 5 copies to the stock level.
my $cost = $book->sell(2); # Take 2 from stock and return
cost
my $price = $book->price(); # Price query
my $stock = $book->stock(); # Stock query
```

3. Run the following script against your class:

```
#!/usr/bin/perl -w
use strict;
use BookLine;
my @info = ();
foreach my $ask ("Title", "Author", "Price", "Stock") {
    print "Enter $ask: ";
    my $input = <STDIN>;
    chomp $input;
    push @info, $input;
}
my $book = new BookLine(@info);
print "Purchase how many copies? ";
my $purchase = <STDIN>;
chomp $purchase;
my $cost = $book->sell($purchase);
print "Cost of $purchase books: \$" . $cost . "\n";
print "Stock remaining: " . $book->stock() . "\n";
```

Summary

As you can see from the examples you have just written, Perl's Object Oriented programming framework is very simple. Like most languages that have been around a while, these concepts have been grafted on later (in Perl's case, version 5.0 was the first to have Object Oriented facilities built into the language).

Perl's facilities are somewhat unique when compared to other languages like C++ and Java. Having no specific constructor allows the name of the constructor to be better aligned to the actual task, even if the vast majority of modules use the new function as their constructor. As well, having no private internal functions means that any of your functions can be called from outside, which can increase complexity.

We will extend the ideas of classes in the next topic when we talk about the concept of "tieing" variables to classes.

Review Questions

1. What is the name of the destructor in Perl?

   _____

   _____

   _____

   _____

   _____

2. Name some ways that Perl's OO implementations differs from another language that you know.

   _____

   _____

   _____

   _____

   _____

Topic 10 – Databases and Perl

Overview

In is topic we will cover connecting to a data source to extract and report on data, as well as to provide simple persistence to data structures. In addition, we look at connecting Perl to larger databases for access to relational databases such as MySQL and others.

Topic Objectives

At the end of this topic, you will be able to:

- Connect to a database from within Perl and execute queries

- Interpret the output of select queries in multiple forms, and understand the usefulness of each method.

- Understand the basic layout of Perls database connectivity DBI module suite.

Introduction

This topic covers how Perl handles access to two different types of data. The first is a data store, such as a DBM data store. The other is access to a relational database. For the purpose of the examples we will be using the MySQL database, purely because it is easily accessible, free for most uses and easy to set up[17].

Tie

Before we cover data stores, we need to cover another topic, which is how to tie variables. This is possibly a weird concept for most programmers, as it abstracts away many things.

At a basic level, using `tie` on a variable binds it to a particular class in a different way to the packages we have seen in the previous topic. When you tie a variable, you change it from being a normal scalar, array or hash into being an interface. Here is the basic function call to tie a variable (in this example, a scalar) to a class:

```
my $scalar;
tie $scalar, PerlPackage;
```

At this point, the scalar is tied to the fictional class "PerlPackage". Now say we want to print out the scalar value using this:

```
print $scalar;
```

The first instinct here is to think that it will print an undefined value, as we didn't define `$scalar` to have a value. But instead, the function `PerlPackage::FETCH` is called, and the return value of the function is what will be printed out. For example, it may look like this:

```
Package PerlPackage;
sub FETCH {
        return int(rand(100));
}
```

So in this case, each time there is an attempt to read `$scalar`, a random number from $0 - 100$ will appear to be stored in the scalar. Note that the FETCH function is called each time the scalar is accessed, so the following:

```
Print "$scalar\n$scalar\n";
```

This would result in 2 different numbers being printed, as the FETCH function is called twice.

When writing the package you want to tie a scalar to, you must implement the following functions:

- TIESCALAR classname, LIST

- FETCH this

- STORE this, value

- DESTROY this

Each of these functions serves a purpose within the scalar. FETCH and STORE are reasonably obvious in that they fetch and store a value when the scalar is read or written to. TIESCALAR is essentially a constructor that builds access to the scalar value. Similarly DESTROY is the destructor, which is called by the garbage collector when the variable is no longer required.

---

[17] To download, please visit http://www.mysql.com and download the community edition for your platform of choice.

Using `tie` on arrays requires a couple of changes to the function list. First of all, `FETCH` and `STORE` now also have a key passed to them. There are also the functions `FETCHSIZE` and `CLEAR`, which return the size of the array and empty the array respectively.

DBM data stores

The reason that we covered `tie` just now is that one of the uses for it is to bind a hash against a persistent storage. DBM data stores provide a convenient means of storing data in a hash to a persistent location. The advantage here is that there is no requirement to read this data in from an external source each time.

A DBM data store is essentially a means of storing a set of data in an easily accessible fashion. It does not implement the kind of functionality you would see in a relational database, as they handle multiple tables and can cross link between them. A data store is effectively the means to store a single table at best, and provide a single means of searching (which is in this case the hash element). Whilst it is possible to perform more complex searching on these data stores, it usually requires additional programming either in the form of Perl modules or other additional code libraries.

To create a connection to a DBM data store, you need to first know which is implemented in your system, as the DBM backend is often system dependent. SDBM is a substitute DBM implementation that is platform independent and is compiled with Perl by default. Whilst there are other implementations such as GDBM, NDBM and others that perhaps have more useful features, SDBM is good enough for most uses.

To create the initial `tie`, we supply a few extra arguments to the `tie` call:

```perl
my %hash;
tie(%hash, 'SDBM_File', "datafile" , O_RDWR|O_CREAT, 0640);
```

At this point, you will have access to the data store in "`datafile`" via `%hash`. You can access elements of the hash as you normally would, ie:

```perl
foreach my $key (sort keys %hash) {
    print "$key -> $hash{$key}\n";
}
```

This would read each hash element from the data store and print it out to the screen. Similarly, statements like these:

```
$hash{'key'} = "hello";
$hash{'key2'} = "This is a value";
$hash{'blah'} = $hash{'key'} . " " . $name;
```

will store data away in the data store for later use either later in this script or when you run the script at a later stage.

One inherent weakness in the SDBM implementation is that it only stores up to 1 kilobyte (1024 chars) in each entry of the database. That includes both key and value. So you may well run into issues for larger data. The one advantage it has is that it is the one DBM implementation that is guaranteed to exist and have Perl modules available for it on any installation of Perl.

Exercise 10.2 – Connecting to a DBM data store.

1. Create a script name ex-10.2.pl which attaches a hash named %hash to a DBM store using SDBM_File. Use the examples above if you need help.

2. Once attached to the hash, run this code several times:

    ```
    $hash{'test'} = $hash{'counter'};
    $hash{'counter'}++;
    $hash{'big'} = ($hash{'counter'} * $hash{'big'}) + 1;

    foreach my $key (sort keys %hash) {
        print "$key = $hash{$key}\n";
    }
    ```

Databases and Perl

Now that we have gotten around some of the ideas of connecting to external data, let's look at something a bit more complicated – a database. For the purposes of these exercises, we will be looking primarily at connecting to a MySQL database, but Perl has libraries for connecting to a large number of databases. And here's the beauty of Perl's database connection implementation – it's mostly the same between different databases.

The reason for this is that Perl abstracts the database connection away from your scripts via a module called DBI. The DBI Perl module is a database independent method of connecting to and working with a database. Database drivers provide the actual database-dependent connections to the database you are working with. These database drivers are named DBD::*DatabaseName*, replacing DatabaseName with the name of the database you want to connect to. You may need to install a database driver for the particular database you need to connect to.

To connect to a database, you use the connect function like this:

```
my $dbh = DBI->connect($data_source, $username, $auth, \%attr);
```

In this example, the scalar $data_source contains information about what database we want to connect to. For a MySQL database, this would be "DBI:mysql:database=dbname;host=hostname". There are 2 encoded pieces of information in here. The first is a colon separated list of information containing the information DBI needs, the second is information required by the database driver for configuring its connection to the database. In the case of MySQL, this is a semi-colon separated list of information that DBD::mysql requires to connect to the database you need on the MySQL server.

Next is the $username and $auth scalars, which provide any authentication information that is required to access the data source. Some data sources will not require this, but most will. So we put a username into $username and an $auth contains an authentication string (which is whatever is required for the database connector you are using).

So a more complete example of a login could be:

```
my $dbh = DBI->connect("DBI:mysql:database=test;hostname=localhost", "user",
"password");
```

We can test that the connection was successful using something like this:

```
if (! $dbh) {
    die $DBI::errstr;
}
```

The scalar $DBI::errstr is the error string for what is wrong either from DBI or from the database driver, whichever raised the connection problem.

Now that we have (we hope) a connection to the database, we can start to run queries on the database using 2 functions – prepare and execute.

The prepare function is the function you pass your query statement to, in the case of MySQL (and most other data sources), this comes in the form of an SQL statement. This will prepare the query for execution, but will not actually run it. It returns a scalar object which contains the query. Executing the query requires taking that scalar and running the execute function on it. So if we have a table named "customers", we could run a query on the table to grab out all customers:

```
my $query = $dbh->prepare("SELECT * FROM customers");
$query->execute();
```

Inside the object in $query, we have an executed query, as well as the results of that query. We can extract information about the query using some of these functions:

```
my $rows = $query->rows(); # Number of rows in the query result

$dbh->commit();   # Commit the changes (if transactional database)
$dbh->rollback(); # Rollback the database (if transactional database)
```

Now we can retrieve the database results. To do this, we use any of the following functions:

```
my $hashref = $query->fetchrow_hashref;
my $arr_ref = $query->fetchrow_arrayref;

my $allhash = $query->fetchall_hashref;
my $allarr  = $query->fetchall_arrayref;
```

We will only look at the fetchrow_hashref function in this example. The fetching by array reference means that we don't get any information about which data is in which element. If we want to go through each row in turn, we can do this easily with a while loop like this:

```
while (my $hashref = $query->fetchrow_hashref) {
    # Work with each row in turn.
}
```

Remember here that the while loop will return false when there is no longer any rows to read from the results set. Each hash element contains one row. The keys contain the names of each data column; the values contain the corresponding values for that row.

Here is an example that puts everything together:

```perl
my $dbh = DBI->connect("DBI:mysql:database=test;hostname=localhost",
                "user", "password");
if (! $dbh) {
    die $DBI::errstr;
}
my $query = $dbh->prepare("SELECT * FROM customers");
$query->execute() or die "Unable to execute query!\n";
while (my $href = $query->fetchrow_hashref) {
    foreach my $key (sort keys %{$href}) {
        print "$key:\t$href->{$key}\n";
    }
}
$query->finish();       # Finish using this query.
$dbh->disconnect();     # Disconnect from database.
```

The last 2 function calls are not strictly necessary; basically they clean up the database connection. The garbage collector in Perl will call these functions if you don't.

Of course you can also run UPDATE, DELETE and other SQL commands through the same function calls. In the case of functions like these, there is obviously not the requirement to fetch rows, and the rows() function call returns the number of rows affected by the function call (i.e. Running the SQL command 'DELETE' then running rows() will return the number of rows that were deleted.)

One issue with SQL statements and any programming language interface is that if you want to use input from a user there is the potential for it to interfere with the execution of the query. For example, if we wanted to search for a particular customer, we could have the code:

```perl
print "Enter the name: ";
my $name = <STDIN>;
chomp $name;
# Note we have escaped the double quotes so that they stay in the string.
my $query = $dbh->prepare("SELECT * FROM customers WHERE name=\"$name\"");
#... continue with processing the query
```

If the user types a double quote when typing in the name, this will result in a fault in the execution of the query. Worse still, the user can perform something called "Code injection", which means that they can get their own SQL statement to be executed in addition. For example, typing in the following would be disastrous:

```
Enter the name: "; DELETE FROM customers;
```

The solution to this is to use a function provided within DBI called quote. This function will quote any character that could interfere with the execution of the query. It's a simple matter of doing this instead:

```perl
print "Enter the name: ";
my $name = <STDIN>;
chomp $name;
my $qname = $dbh->query($name);
my $query = $dbh->prepare("SELECT * FROM customers WHERE name=$qname");
#... continue with processing the query
```

In this case, the values are also placed inside double quotes if they are strings or not if they are numeric. The function call ensures that data is safe for use in an SQL statement.

Exercise 10.3 – Data validation and more complex database communications

Note: This exercise assumes that you have set up a MySQL database with the sample tables.

Write a Perl script named ex-10.3.pl that:

1. Connects to the MySQL database using connection information supplied by your instructor.

2. Verifies the connection and provides a connection error message if it doesn't work

3. Performs the following query and prints the resulting tables:

   ```
   SELECT * FROM Aircraft;
   ```

4. In a second script, ex-10.4.pl, connect to the MySQL database and insert a row into the Aircraft table of the database. This is the data structure for the Aircraft:

   ```
   Id            INT UNSIGNED PRIMARY KEY,
   Manufacturer VARCHAR(30),
   Model         VARCHAR(30),
   Purchased     DATE,
   LastChecked   DATETIME
   ```

Summary

We have now looked at a few of the means that Perl has to connect to persistent storage. We have looked at DBM hashes in the form of SDBM_File (and others), which provide a means of tieing a variable to a class, which in turn ties it to a persistent data store.

We have now also seen Perl's flexible system for attaching to databases. Whilst we have only looked at connecting to a MySQL database, Perl will happily connect to a large number of other databases such as Oracle™ and others.

Review Questions

1. Briefly describe the layout of Perl's DBI module set.

    _____

    _____

    _____

    _____

    _____

2. What other possible data stores can you think of that could be used in a tied environment?

    _____

    _____

    _____

    _____

    _____

Topic 11 – Debugging Perl and writing better code

Overview

In this topic, we cover the used of the Perl debugger and other debugging resources available within Perl. We also review some of the areas where Perl code can be harder to maintain and provide some ideas about writing more maintainable code.

Topic Objectives

At the end of this topic, you will be able to:

- Debug Perl scripts using the internal Perl debugger

- Understand other debugging resources within Perl

- Understand some techniques that can be used to improve Perl code to be more maintainable.

Debugging Perl Code

Software written in any computer programming language needs to be debugged. Most commonly used languages such as C, C++ and Java have had many tools written to assist the process of writing reliable code. Perl has some advantages over a lot of these languages in that there are already some strong debugging tools written into the language. In addition, there is the advantage that Perl has existed long enough to have had some more comprehensive debugging tools made to be part of the language, as well as incorporate some features into the interpreter to assist with debugging.

Some of the ideas for aiding debugging code we have covered already, but we will cover them again here for completeness.

The first is the use of the command line switch -w. The -w switch enables additional warnings in the interpreter. The most common issue that this will pick up is when you try and use a value that hasn't been defined in places where it should be defined (for example, adding two values together when only one of them is defined). In addition, this will pick up when you are trying to read from a file handle that is closed or at end of file.

The second we have looked at is the use of the strict module. When we covered that back in topic 4 we primarily looked at how it forced us to define a scope for any variable we want to use, but it's also useful for ensuring that references and subroutines behave in a consistent fashion. Using the strict module will generate additional compile time errors if you attempt to use bare word identifiers that are not subroutines or other parts of the Perl language where you shouldn't.

In addition, the strict module removes the ability to use symbolic references, which stop you from being able to do things like this:

```
$variable = "hello"
$string = "variable"; # name of a variable we want to print.
print $$string;
```

Doing the same thing without symbolic references requires the use of eval, which evaluates a given Perl expression:

```
$variable = "hello";
$string = "variable";
eval "print \$$string";
```

There are some other Perl modules that assist both with writing more readable code but also with debugging your programs. Here are some others:

```
use English;
```

Using the English module adds English names to Perls' internal variables. For example, $ERRNO is available instead of $!, $EVAL_ERROR is available for $@ and so on. Refer to the perlvar manpage for a full list. This means that instead of this:

```
open FH, $file or die "Unable to open $file: $!\n";
```

It is possible to have the more readable:

```
open FH, $file or die "Unable to open $file: $ERRNO\n";
```

Perl Debugger

The Perl debugger is perhaps one of the most useful ways of finding out exactly what your Perl script is doing and why. It works like any other debugger you may have seen for languages like C or Java in that it allows you to step through your script at key points and interrogate the Perl interpreter to understand what your script is doing.

The Perl debugger is initiated by running the Perl interpreter with the –d command line flag, which means that it is easy to debug any Perl script on any system where you have Perl installed – no additional software is necessary. When you start up the debugger, you will get something like the following:

```
Loading DB routines from perl5db.pl version 1.28
Editor support available.

Enter h or `h h' for help, or `man perldebug' for more help.

main::(test.pl:13):    my %opts = ();

  DB<1>
```

The DB<1> bit is a prompt for what to do. Options include stepping to the next command, setting breakpoints and so on. Here is a table with the commonly used keys when using the debugger:

Command	Effect
n	Step to next command
s	Step into function call (works same as n if no function call
r	Return from current subroutine
l *num*	List out a particular line of code
c *num*	Continue execution until script reaches this line number.
b *num*	Set a break point at a particular line number.
B *num*	Remove a break point at a particular line number
R	Restart the script
h	Print a help screen.
T	Print the current stack trace (list of functions where the script is currently in)
q	Quit

Table 8 - Perl Debugger Commands

As you step through your script, the debugger will print out each line before you execute it (unless you tell it to continue to a later part of the script). You also have the option to run Perl commands to manipulate the environment, conditions, etc. You can also use the Perl commands to interrogate what the system thinks the current state is, including the current contents of scalar values and so forth. A common command to use here would be the print statement, and getting it to print out the current value of a scalar, array or hash.

Exercise 11.1 – Perl Debugger

1. Bring up the Perl debugger using 'perl -d script' for a script you have written today (A good and complex example would be any of the scripts written with the Object Oriented programming topic, particularly exercise 9.2). Bring up the help for the debugger to understand what each command can do.

   Now step through the script using 's' to step into subroutines you want to look into (remember that it will also step into subroutines you didn't write, so you may want to use 'n' for those to skip over them)

Common Perl Mistakes

There are a number of mistakes that people who are new to programming with Perl often make. Chances are you have done a couple of these while writing your own scripts to answer exercises for this book. Here are some of the common mistakes that people make when writing Perl scripts:

Forgetting that printing to a file handle means you don't put a comma between the file handle and the data. This one is very common. Quite often you will write code like this:

```
print FH, $data;        # WRONG!

print FH $data;         # CORRECT
```

Similarly, you will often go the other way when opening a file and *forget* to put a comma in when it's needed. For example:

```
open FH ">$filename";    # WRONG

open FH, ">$filename";   # CORRECT
```

Relying on PATH environment variable when executing commands. This is a common flaw when you will rely upon a users PATH environment to locate an executable. This should never happen, as you can never rely on a users PATH environment to include what you want it to include. And even if it does include what you want, it may not be in the right order.

This is especially true on UNIX hosts where there are multiple implementations of the same command, like on Solaris for example. There are 4-5 implementations of the grep command, for example, and each behaves *slightly* differently to the other. If you are relying on the version of grep that is in /usr/bin, but a users' path includes /usr/xpg4/bin in their path before /usr/bin, your script may not work correctly.

The solution to this is to always put the full path to any external command, file or other resource you intend to use. In the case of commands, often what will be the best way to deal with this is to do something like this:

```
my $GREP = "/usr/bin/grep";

my @user = `${GREP} user /etc/passwd`;
```

This way, you ensure that the version of `grep` that is run is the one you want, and will behave in the manner you expect. Also note that the location of grep you want may differ on different types of systems. For example:

```
my $system = `/usr/bin/uname -s`;
chomp $system;
my ($GREP, $LS);
$LS = '/bin/ls';
if ($system eq 'SunOS') {
        $GREP = '/usr/xpg4/bin/grep';
} elsif ($system eq 'HP-UX') {
        $GREP = '/usr/bin/grep';
}
```

Here the `ls` command is known to be in the same place for both Solaris and HP-UX. However the `grep` command that we want is in a different location on Solaris to HP-UX so we have to set it on a system-by-system basis so that our script will behave the way we are expecting.

Semicolons are required at the end of all Perl statements. It is a common thing to forget if you have been writing shell scripts or with other languages that don't use line terminators like semi-colons.

Perl requires semi-colons at the end of all statements, with one exception – they are not required on the last command in a block. For example, the following is actually legal:

```
if ($a > 5) {
        print "This is weird, but legal"
}
```

However, it is probably easier and makes the code more readable to put semi-colons at the end of all statements.

Comparisons between scalars are either numerical or string. Its important to remember that == does a numerical comparison, while `eq` does a string comparison. It is quite common to forget this, which will result in error messages like:

```
Argument "string" isn't numeric in numeric eq (==) at myscript line 25.
```

If you see something like this, then you are attempting to do a numerical comparison on a string. You need to use `eq`, `ne`, `gt` or `lt` instead.

Curly brackets are required for all conditional and loop constructs. Unlike in C, where conditions with a single line are executed, in Perl scripts you must put braces for every conditional. This means that you cannot do this:

```
if ($a > 5) print "A is greater than 5"; # ILLEGAL

if (a > 5) {
        print "A is greater than 5"; # LEGAL
}
```

Of course, Perl does allow you to do these things in reverse:

```
print "A is greater than 5" if ($a > 5); # ALSO LEGAL
```

Some functions behave differently in scalar and list contexts. Some functions do slightly different things depending on what type of value it is returning to. For example:

```
$date = localtime();
print $date;          # Tue Jul 31 18:03:31 2007
@date = localtime();
print join(", ", @date); # 31, 3, 18, 31, 6, 107, 2, 211, 0
```

As you can see, when `localtime()` returns to a scalar, it returns a string version of the current time. When it returns to an array, it breaks the information up into elements that can be manipulated more easily.

In addition, reading from a file handle behaves differently if you are reading to an array compared to a scalar. If you are reading to a scalar, only the first record is read (up to the next "\n"). If reading to an array, then the rest of the file is read into the array, one element per entry (usually one line of text per element).

Return code from some system calls can be misleading. Calls to functions like `system()` can give misleading return values. This is because additional information in the form of which signals were sent to the process to terminate it. If you want to actually figure out the return code of a process from a system call:

```
system($command);
my $returncode = $? >> 8;
```

If you want to check for all possible issues from a system call, use this:

```
if ($? == -1) {
    print "failed to execute: $!\n";
} elsif ($? & 127) {
    print "Died with signal " . ($? & 127) . "\n";
    print "(Core dumped)\n" if ($? & 128);
} else {
    print "Exited with value " . ($? >> 8) . "\n";
}
```

Writing test code for Perl Modules and Scripts

Writing robust code is one thing. Testing that code is another. One of the nicer features that have come to be part of the set of modules available with Perl is the ability to write programming-level test cases to verify code does not get broken once written.

The Perl module 'Test' is a small start in terms of writing test cases for your scripts. It is reasonably easy to use – you simply put each test into its own function call. Here is an example:

```
#!/usr/bin/perl -w
use strict;
use Test;

BEGIN { plan tests => 5 }

# Some test data
$a = 2;
$b = 5;
$c = 3;

ok( $a == 0 );
ok( $c > $b );
ok( $a < $b );
ok( $a + $c == $b );
ok( $b * 2 > 50);
```

Let's dissect this script briefly before running it. The inclusion of the Test module requires that we know how many tests we are going to run. If you don't know how many tests you are going to run, you will need to figure it out before you attempt to run any tests. Usually, that means putting in some checks into a BEGIN code block, so that this way we are able to verify exactly how many tests are to be run.

Each call to ok() represents one test. There is another call that can be made for tests – skip, which we will cover shortly.

When executing this script, you will get the following:

```
1..5
# Running under perl version 5.008007
# Current time local: Sun Aug  5 18:47:02 2007
# Current time GMT:   Sun Aug  5 08:47:02 2007
# Using Test.pm version 1.25
not ok 1
# Failed test 1 in a at line 12
#   a line 12 is: ok( $a == 0 );
not ok 2
# Failed test 2 in a at line 13
#   a line 13 is: ok( $c > $b );
ok 3
ok 4
not ok 5
# Failed test 5 in a at line 16
#   a line 16 is: ok( $b * 2 > 50);
```

This provides a standard report about what tests passed, failed or were skipped. Tests can be skipped under certain conditions if the test script allows them to be skipped. Let's say we added in another test into the above script. After changing the number of tests in the BEGIN block, we add the following line of code at the end:

```
skip( $a < 5, $a == 10 );
```

This example means that we will skip the test if $a is less than 5. A skipped test is registered as passed. Perl defines a skip test as basically:

```
if ( skipcondition ) {
        ok(1);
} else {
        ok(test);
}
```

> **Exercise 11.2 – Writing test scripts**
>
> 1. Write a test script using Perl's internal Test module to test your BookLine module. Write tests that ensure that each function works as you expect it to work.
>
> 2. Introduce an inconsistency into your module (say for example you make the stock function return an incorrect value) and observe the difference in output from the Test module.

Summary

This topic has been primarily about how to write better code. Perl provides some assistance in the form of debuggers, test harnesses, etc. however ultimately the responsibility for writing good code rests with the author of the code.

As you can see from the common errors that have been shown here, most of the common mistakes are easily corrected, provided you are aware of them. Using modules such as `strict`, `warnings` and so on assist with picking up many of these errors.

Please note, while the test harness in Perl is complete enough for basic test harnesses, there are other modules that exist on CPAN[18] that will expand the capabilities of test harnesses.

---

[18] We will cover CPAN in topic 13 shortly.

Review Questions

1. Reviewing the common mistakes mentioned, what common themes can you see?

_____

_____

_____

_____

_____

2. In the Perl debugger, how do you set a breakpoint?

_____

_____

_____

_____

_____

Topic 12 – Documenting Perl code using Perldoc

Overview

This section will show you how to write user documentation inline with your Perl code in a format known as "perldoc". Perldoc is a way of writing documentation that is then convertible to formats such as HTML, man pages and so forth.

Topic Objectives

At the end of this topic, you will be able to:

- Write inline documentation inside your Perl code

- Use utilities such as perldoc, pod2html, etc. to produce usable documentation

POD Documentation

Most developers hate documentation. So therefore when programmers think about what documentation they should do, there is an attempt to either make it as simple as possible so as not to be overly useful, or there is an attempt to make it as simple as possible to do, so that its more likely that a semi-decent job of it will be done.

This is especially an issue for any code where there is not a corporate influence, such as in the open source community.

As a result, Perl was one of the first languages to attempt to perform in-code documentation. This is not commenting code, which you should already know. This is embedding documentation in the code that it relates to. The hope here is that the documentation will be updated as you update the code. The language Perl uses here is called POD (Plain Old Documentation).

As a short exercise, run this command:

```
$ perldoc Net::FTP
```

Actually, you could run this on **any** Perl module. What you get is documentation about how to use this module. Take a moment to read through it so that you get a feel for the type of information that is present, and how it is generally set out.

Now that you can see how useful this could be, let's take a look at how you would write your own.

The basics

Essentially, paragraphs in POD are like paragraphs of text. Separate paragraphs by a blank line. For example:

```
Paragraph 1

Paragraph 2
```

Within a paragraph you can make specific text bold, underlined, etc. You do this using a set of formatting codes. Here are a few examples:

```
B<Bold Text>
I<Italics Text>
C<Code Text>
```

There are several others, have a look at the `perlpod` man page for the full set.

Of course, putting in paragraphs of text in the middle of your code is going to be difficult to distinguish between text and code that is intended to be Perl code, especially if your documentation contains Perl code. As a result, any POD documentation must begin with a POD command, which is probably more like a markup in something like HTML.

Commands in POD handle some of the formatting and structure of the documentation. For example, you have heading commands, indent commands (and the reverse), commands for bullet lists and so on. It doesn't matter which one you use, a common trick is to use the bullet point command to document an individual function before the actual function itself.

POD documentation does not need to be all in one big block; it is possible to break it up into many small blocks inside your code. This has the advantage of allowing you to document the code right next to where the code happens to be.

Sample POD documentation

Let's have a look at some sample POD documentation. This is the first section of code from the Net::FTP module:

```
=head1 NAME

Net::FTP - FTP Client class

=head1 SYNOPSIS

    use Net::FTP;

    $ftp = Net::FTP->new("some.host.name", Debug => 0)
      or die "Cannot connect to some.host.name: $@";

    $ftp->login("anonymous",'-anonymous@')
      or die "Cannot login ", $ftp->message;

    $ftp->cwd("/pub")
      or die "Cannot change working directory ", $ftp->message;

    $ftp->get("that.file")
      or die "get failed ", $ftp->message;

    $ftp->quit;

=head1 DESCRIPTION

C<Net::FTP> is a class implementing a simple FTP client in Perl as
described in RFC959.  It provides wrappers for a subset of the RFC959
commands.
```

At the start, you can see the headings being set out. This will cause the heading to look like this:

```
NAME
        Net::FTP - FTP Client class
```

As you can see, the text for the actual heading is not exactly the heading here. This is a convention that Perl modules use. It's not essential that you use this convention for your own documentation, but any modules you write for CPAN must have documentation in this format.

Making lists

Lists in POD are quite simple, you use =over and =back as the start and end marks respectively, and =item is used for each item in the list.

Essentially, =over indents the left margin for a while. A number is specified to the command to say how far over we should go, while =back returns the left margin to where it was prior to the =over call. Here is a simple example:

```
=over 5

=item This is the item

=item This is another item

=back
```

Bulleted items can be done like this:

```
=item *

Item text
```

And numbered items can be done like this: (Remember to keep track of the order, POD doesn't):

```
=item 1.

Item text
```

Finishing up POD and getting on with code

Remember how we mentioned that POD can be split up and put inside code? Well, we have told you how to start a section of POD, but we haven't yet told you how to finish it. Here is how:

```
=item function()

Definition of function.

=cut

sub function {
      ...
```

As you can see, the =cut command tells us that we are at the end of this section of POD documentation. From this point we can continue Perl coding as normal.

Viewing and formatting your code

Writing the documentation into your code is all well and good, but you need the tools to extract it and place it into a viewable format. Perl provides a number of tools for this. The first one we have already seen a couple of times: `perldoc`.

The perldoc command is used to extract the POD documentation, format it and display the output to screen using a pager like 'more'. It will search through Perl's runtime library include list to find the modules documentation, but you can also specify a particular file that you want to extract the documentation from.

The other commands relate to converting POD into other formats. To do this, there are 5 commands that are available to use: `pod2html`, `pod2latex`, `pod2man`, `pod2text` and `pod2usage`. Each will convert the POD documentation to the format mentioned, HTML, LaTeX, Man page, raw text or a special one that creates usage statements for use in your code.

To convert the documentation, simply run the command like this:

```
% pod2html module > text.html
```

By default, the HTML output is displayed to the screen, so a redirection is essential if you want to save the results to a file. The HTML documentation is capable of cross linking between modules, and command line options can be given to ensure that these cross links go to the correct place, such as:

```
% pod2html --htmlroot=http://www.yoursite.com/docs module > text.html
```

Exercise 12.1 – Writing documentation with Perldoc

1. Take the `BookLine` module from exercise 9.2 and add in POD documentation to it, documenting each function. Use examples from both this text and the layout of other modules you have seen to assist you.

2. Run 'perldoc `BookLine.pm`' to view the documentation in a manpage style.

3. Run 'pod2html `BookLine.pm` > `BookLine.html`' to generate HTML documentation for your module.

Summary

Documentation is something that programmers of any discipline have a tendency to avoid. Providing a mechanism to assist with the process of documenting code has become an essential part of many languages, and Perl was one of the first languages to implement a feature like this. Java programmers may be familiar with the Javadoc system for documenting code; however POD is perhaps a more flexible system that does not add too much additional complexity.

Review Questions

1. How do you end a block of POD documentation?

    _____

    _____

    _____

    _____

    _____

2. What sorts of documentation would you put into POD documentation for a script?

    _____

    _____

    _____

    _____

    _____

Topic 13 – CPAN – Comprehensive Perl Archive Network.

Overview

The Comprehensive Perl Archive Network is a site on the internet that compiles a large collection of Perl modules that are available for use with your Perl scripts. Perl comes with a command line utility that can assist with adding in these modules.

Topic Objectives

At the end of this topic, you will be able to:

- Understand the type and volume of available code

- Install modules from CPAN in either Windows or Unix

- Write code that uses some of these modules

CPAN – What does it contain?

The *"Comprehensive Perl Archive Network"* (CPAN) is a repository of Perl code that is available to assist with your programming requirements. It exists at http://www.cpan.org. It contains:

- Perl modules

- Perl scripts

We will focus primarily on the modules that are available within CPAN, as they are by far the most useful resource available on the website. At time of writing, there were approx. 11,000 Perl modules contained in the archive, and more are added on a regular basis. They cover a wide variety of things, from mathematical calculation code to graphical user interfaces.

The CPAN module

One module that comes with Perl is the CPAN module. This module provides a programming level interface to installing and maintaining modules from the CPAN archive. In its simplest incarnation, we can get it to start up a command line shell:

```
$ perl -MCPAN -e shell
```

This command line execution will run Perl and start up a CPAN shell. In more recent releases of Perl, this has been placed into a simple command: 'cpan'.

Exercise 13.1 – Installing modules from CPAN

1. Start up the CPAN shell.

2. Run through the configuration, using the defaults for everything – check if your environment requires the use of a proxy. If so, make sure that information is entered in at the appropriate time. Remember to select an archive mirror that is located near you.

3. Once you are at the cpan shell, run the following:

    ```
    cpan> i /Mail::/
    cpan> install Mail::Send
    ... (Watch the output, it should indicate if it was
    successful
    or not)
    ```

4. Quit the CPAN shell and test that the module you imported is installed:

    ```
    % perl -Mmail::Send -e print
    ```

Some modules from Core Perl and CPAN

We will now have a look at some of the modules that are found both in the Perl distribution and in CPAN. In the case of the CPAN modules, you will need to install them before you can use them.

We are going to have a look at 3 modules. From the internal Perl distribution, we are going to look at `Getopt::Std`, which is a means of simplifying command line parsing. We will also look at `LWP`, from the `libwww` set of modules in CPAN. This provides Perl with the ability to access websites. Finally we will look at a somewhat odd Perl module named `Acme::Ook`, which provides a source filter to allow you to write programs in the Ook programming language.

Getopt::Std – Parsing the command line

The Getopt::Std Perl module is a handy module that comes with the Perl distribution. Its purpose is to provide a standard mechanism for handling command line switches.

When it is imported, the module exports two functions to the calling namespace – `getopt` and `getopts`. These behave largely in the same way that they behave with the C library of the same name. The getopt function just handles flags – they can be either on or off. The `getopts` function allows flags to take values, for example:

```
% ./myscript.pl -c -v 3
```

Using `getopts`, you can request that the c and v flags are desirable, and to allow v to take an argument.

The `Getopts::Std` module informs you of which options are selected in either of two ways, either by defining variables such as `$opt_c` for checking if option `-c` has been selected, or by storing it all in a hash. Here is some example code for working with getopts:

```
use Getopt::Std;

my %opts;
getopts("cv:", \%opts);
print "C: $opts{'c'} V: $opts{'v'}\n";
```

In this case, we have defined an empty hash, passed it as a *reference* to the `getopts` function, which will check for options c and v. Finally, we print out the values for each option so we can see what values they were given.

It's important to note that getopts will only process the flags you are looking for. If we were to pass this script say the '-h' option, it would not resulting `$opts{'h'}` being set. Furthermore, it would result in the following warning being displayed:

```
Unknown option: h
```

The other point to note is that any of the options not set will be undefined, so running that code above any options not defined will result in a warning about using uninitialized values.

LWP – Downloading website

The next module we are going to look at is LWP. This module (actually a set of modules) provides us with the ability to use Perl as if it were a browser. Specifically, it allows us to make use of the HTTP protocol.

This module doesn't come with Perl by default, so you will need to install it. Here is how:

```
$ perl -MCPAN -e 'install libwww'
```

If you are using the ActiveState™ version of Perl, you can download it via the Perl Package Manager GUI. It is possible it will require a few other modules such as URI and others; you will need to install those as well in order to use LWP.

Once you install it, here is some sample code to download a URL:

```
#!/usr/bin/perl -w
use strict;
use LWP;
my $ua = new LWP::UserAgent;
$ua->agent("My Perl Script/1"); # Browser identification string
my $request = new HTTP::Request(GET => "http://www.google.com");
my $response = $ua->request($request);
if ($response->is_success()) {
        print $response->content;
} else {
        print $response->status_line . "\n";
}
```

OK. Let's step through that code, as there is a fair amount in there. First section is to perform some package imports. Note we haven't imported HTTP::Request here (which is used later on). Thankfully, LWP imports a few other modules for us as a convenience, this one included.

After that, we create a new LWP::UserAgent. This is the package that does the actual requesting. Think of it as your web browser. It performs the actual HTTP transport for your request. Next we have to create an actual request. Perl has a module for doing this, HTTP::Request. This would have been installed when you installed the libwww package in CPAN. We pass the URL to the request that we want, and an object is created for us to perform our request.

Next we pass the request to the user agent. This performs the actual download of the URL we requested. It stores the response in the form of an object from the HTTP::Response class. This one is also included with libwww.

Now that we have attempted our request, the response variable tells us what (if anything) came back from the server. The function call to $response->is_success() checks if the response from the server indicated success. For that to be the case, the response from the server must have been in the 200 class responses. Responses such as 404 (file not found) and 500 (internal error) will result in this function returning a false value.

Finally, the two functions content and status_line pull out specific parts of the HTTP response. The content function pulls out the actual data content, while status_line pulls out the response code (ie. 404) and what it means (ie. File not found).

Acme::Ook – Not every Perl module needs to be serious...

Not all of the modules in CPAN are serious, however. Any module that begins with the name 'Acme::' is more often than not humorous in nature. For example there is the package Acme::Ook, which implements the Ook[19] programming language.

One interesting point to note with the Acme:: set of modules is that they quite often implement some of the more interesting language features. In the case of the Acme::Ook module, it implements a feature called source filtering. Essentially what it does is that it allows you to translate your code in some form prior to execution. The module Acme::Ook translates Ook code into Perl code which then allows the interpreter to run the code.

So let's look at some sample Ook code:

```
#!/usr/bin/perl
use Acme::Ook;
Ook. Ook. Ook! Ook? Ook. Ook? Ook. Ook! Ook? Ook!
Ook? Ook. Ook! Ook! Ook! Ook? Ook. Ook. Ook! Ook.
Ook? Ook. Ook! Ook! Ook? Ook!
```

For reference, the above example prints a file in reverse order. (This example was taken from the Acme::Ook perldoc documentation)

There are a number of source filters on CPAN; most are more useful than this. Some allow a degree of encoding of your Perl code, although these are never truly secure as they must still be translated into executable perl code before execution, and are therefore readable.

---

[19] For more information on the Ook! Programming language, visit http://www.dangermouse.net/esoteric/ook.html

Summary

This topic has given a basic understanding of what CPAN is, and how it can assist with your programming requirements in the form of modules and scripts. At last count, there were over 10,000 separate modules that are available for use; many of these are based around established network protocols, file formats or database connectivity.

It is worth reviewing the list of modules in CPAN to understand exactly what is available. This topic has provided a basic sampling of the available modules; however there are many more that can provide assistance to Perl programmers.

Review Questions

1. How do you install modules from CPAN?

_____

_____

_____

_____

_____

2. Search the CPAN archives, what other test harnesses can you find? (hint: most start with 'Test::')

_____

_____

_____

_____

_____

Topic 14 – Threading in Perl

Overview

In this topic we review an advanced feature of Perl – threading. Perls' threading model allows concurrent execution of Perl code and the ability to both separate and share data between threads. This topic will cover setting up and executing threads within Perl as well as putting together some basic models for running threads in a scripted environment.

Topic Objectives

At the end of this topic, you will be able to:

- Understand the threading model implemented by Perl, including abilities and limitations

- Create Perl scripts that are multi-threaded

- Share data between threads in a Perl script

Using threads

One of the more recent additions to the Perl interpreter has been the ability to run multi-threaded Perl scripts. Whilst the code for this library is considered "experimental", it is included in the stable releases of Perl as an optional add-in at compile time. Perl calls this feature "ithreads", which basically means interpreter threads.

In Perl, each thread has its own interpreter, which keeps the threads apart from one another. Whilst it is possible to share data between threads, for most applications, it is as if a second copy of Perl has been run.

To check if the interpreter you are working with supports threads, run 'perl -V' and look for the compile time options:

```
Compile-time options: MULTIPLICITY USE_ITHREADS USE_64_BIT_INT
                      USE_LARGE_FILES USE_SITECUSTOMIZE
                      PERL_IMPLICIT_CONTEXT
```

If you see 'USE_ITHREADS' here then you have threads available to use. If not, then the Perl interpreter must be recompiled with this option enabled to allow it.

If you have a threaded version of Perl available, you must include the Perl threading library in your code. This is done by using the 'threads' package. There is also a 'threads::shared' package that can be included in order to enable sharing of data between threads.

Some of the important function calls that are used with the threads package are:

new(coderef) – Constructor method for creating a new thread. (Can also be called "create"). Pass a code reference to this function for the code to be executed for this thread.

tid – Thread ID. Returns the ID number for the current thread.

threads->self – Returns an object for the current thread.

$thread->join – join the thread back to the main script.

threads->detach – Detaches the thread from the main process, making it un-joinable.

And for the threads::shared module, there are the additional functions:

share(item) – share a variable between threads.

lock(item) – Lock variable for exclusive use.

Note that you cannot share blessed objects, which means that objects such as network connections can't be shared between threads. In addition, you cannot use array segments (ie. @array[5..8]) to manipulate the contents of the shared element. These are limitations in the current versions of Perl.

Sample threading script

Let's look at writing a simple thread worker script:

```
#!/usr/local/bin/perl -w
use strict;
use threads;
use threads::shared;
```

First up is fairly straightforward, we include both `threads` and `threads::shared`. Since we are going to share a work queue between threads, we need both modules.

```
our $maxthreads = 10;
our @queue = ();
# Share the queue between threads.
share(@queue);
```

Now we set up a constant for the number of threads we want, as well as setting up the queue and sharing it.

```
# Fill up array with stuff for our test.
my $counter = 0;
while ($counter < 1000) {
        push @queue, $counter;
        $counter++;
}
# Need somewhere to store thread objects.
my @threads = ();
$counter = 0;
while ($counter < $maxthreads) {
        # create a new thread.
        $threads[$counter] = threads->new(\&worker);
        $counter++;
}
```

Next we fill up the array with some data to test with, and then create the threads. We do this through the call to `thread->new`. The argument passed to the call to new contain a reference to the code to run for each thread. In our case, it's a subroutine we have called `worker`. Any further arguments passed to this function call are passed to the subroutine and are accessible in the @_ array.

```
sleep 5 if (scalar(threads->list) > 0);
# OK... Time to start waiting for the worker bees
$counter = 0;
while ($counter < $maxthreads) {
        $threads[$counter]->join();
        $counter++;
}
warn "All threads rejoined...\n";
exit;
```

Finally, we use the `$thread->join()` function call to rejoin the threads once they are finished. We need to make sure that all threads finish up before we terminate. The loop ensures that every thread is joined to the main script before we exit. If we don't do this, then the threads will terminate when the exit command is executed at the main

```
sub worker {
        while (1) { # Exiting loop is handled inside the loop...
                my $this;
                LOCK: {
                        lock(@queue);
                        $this = pop(@queue);
                }
                last if (! $this);
                print threads->tid . ": $this\n";
        }
}
```

Now for the worker function. We have a couple of points to cover here. First is the block of code labeled 'LOCK'. Locks in the threading model here provide the thread with sole access to the item being locked; in this case, it's the array @queue. With locks in Perl, there is no unlock function, rather the lock exists while it is in scope. This is why we have a code block surrounding the lock and the work we need to do with the @queue list. As soon as we are done with @queue, we release the lock for other threads to work with.

The only other function call here of interest is the call to `threads->tid`, which returns the id number for the thread. The base thread (the one the script runs from) is thread id 0. The id's for the created threads start counting from 1 onwards.

Basically, the worker function here loops continuously, taking an object each time through the loop. Once there are no more elements to choose from, the loop exits (thanks to the line 'last if (! $this);').

Exercise 14.1 – Threaded Perl Script

1. Enter in the dissected code example from the last section (Starting from the code block that starts with the `#!/usr/bin/perl` line.)

2. Attempt execution of the script. Is there anything to note about the output is printed?

3. Modify the script to add each value to a rolling total for each thread and print it out prior to returning.

Summary

Threaded programs introduce a whole new complexity to how Perl scripts operate. There is no guarantee that one thread will perform its work before another, there are no guarantees that things will happen across threads in the order that is anticipated. It all depends on which threads get time on the CPU and in what order.

That said, threading your script is the only real way to make use of more than a single CPU, which means that it can be a helpful tool for speeding up your Perl script, assuming that the work your script is doing can be threaded.

Review Questions

1. What functions and modules exist to create new threads in Perl?

    _____

    _____

    _____

    _____

    _____

2. How do you sit and wait for a specific thread to finish?

    _____

    _____

    _____

    _____

    _____

3. Review the code written for the exercise in this chapter. This is a worker model. What other models can you think of that could be used for threading Perl scripts?

    _____

    _____

    _____

    _____

    _____

www.ingramcontent.com/pod-product-compliance
Lightning Source LLC
LaVergne TN
LVHW082341070326
832902LV00042B/2700